PORTRAIT OF A LIVING MARSH

PORTRAIT OF A LIVING MARSH
32 INTERNATIONAL ARTISTS VISIT NORTHEAST POLAND

Robin D'Arcy Shillcock

INMERC BV, Wormer / The Netherlands

"We have been telling ourselves the story of what we represent in the land for 40,000 years. At the heart of this story, I think, is a simple abiding belief: it is possible to live wisely on the land, and to live well. And in behaving respectfully toward all that the land contains, it is possible to imagine a stifling ignorance falling away from us."
- Barry Holstun Lopez (from *Arctic Dreams*)

CONTENTS

WWF® World Wide Fund
For Nature

Office of the President

CH-1196 Gland Switzerland
Telephone: (022) 64 91 11
Telex: 419 618 wwf ch
Telefax: (022) 64 54 68

Artists have been using their talents to depict animals, plants and landscapes for thousands of years, and for thousands of years people have admired their work and gained an insight from it into the wonders of the natural world.

The Artists for Nature Foundation has recognised that artists can make a significant contribution to the conservation of nature by conveying the feeling and atmosphere of a scene in a way that is quite unique. With the guidance of the World Wide Fund for Nature (WWF), the ANF chooses sites that are in special need of attention or protection. Through the work that appears in this book, the artists reveal to readers the beauty and particular quality of the Biebrza and Narew marshes in North East Poland. This is an area of low-intensity farming where there is a stable symbiosis between farming and the natural environment. This gives it a special ecological value and I hope very much that this book will help to ensure that this unique area is given the protection it needs to allow it to retain its present status.

Thirty two artists from fourteen countries have generously contributed work to this book; an eloquent testimony to the concern of artists for the future of the natural world.

Registered as:

WWF - Fondo Mondiale per la Natura
WWF - Fondo Mundial para la Naturaleza
WWF - Fonds Mondial pour la Nature
WWF - Welt Natur Fonds
WWF - World Wide Fund For Nature
  (formerly World Wildlife Fund)

President:

HRH The Duke of Edinburgh

Vice President &
Hon. Treasurer: Babar Ali
Vice President: Russell E. Train
Director General: Charles de Haes

INTRODUCTION

"It was not merely a river; it was a history. I listened to its stories. They re-created for me not only a life I had known but a life, as I later knew, that would not return."
- H.E. Bates[1]

My position on top of the ridge created by an ancient glacier gives a better view of the river flowing through numerous waterways in a valley so low and broad that it fades through tones of softening green to an even softer haze of blue trees in the east. Below me, the river's over-flow has caused arabesques of islands, their fresh green dotted with willowscrub and surrounded by patches of water that mirror the sky, adding to the sense of space above the valley, above me - a sky with towering clouds, a sky for soaring flight.

A week ago this was just a map, flat and without mea-ning, now it is laid out before me in a bewildering succes-sion of water and land, a waterscape so tranquil that fora-ging birds are multiplied by their unbroken reflections . Mute swans, a fairly common species, blend with the white reflection of the sky while they feed on waterplants beneath the surface, pulling up dark strands that drip down from their beautifully curved necks. When bathing, their splashing carries far across the waterways and reed-beds, causing the space of the landscape to be sensed in a different way. On the wind thin laments of black terns drift up to me, and the more familiar calls of godwit - here they abound in astounding numbers. A high group of geese comes over, they look like white-fronts, possibly the last of those heading north to breeding places on the Scan-dinavian and Russian tundra.

There are threats to this landscape I've been told. I try in vain to remember what they are. The truth is: I do not want them to surface, they are less important to me now than what my eyes record. All day I sit looking out across the valley, touched by its peace, enveloped by a different kind of light.

Evidence of human presence on the river came by many hours ago: the spiky silhouette of a man standing on a long, narrow boat that glided fluidly with every slow-motion-stroke of the long pole. In reality I am far from being alone; hidden behind my back is a small vil-lage overlooking the river, and all through the day its sounds make me aware of the presence of man: the whine of an axe held to the grindstone, full buckets being drawn from a well, people's voices and the continuous yapping of a dog.

1) *Biebrza near village of Pluty, lower basin. Photo: Wiktor Wolkow.*

Hearing something and expecting curious children, I turn to see instead an old man who has come up to me. He points to my drawing with a hand that is a minute landscape in itself, overlaid by a network of lines and bulging veins, an archeological artefact compared to my own. He gestures to the river and showers me with words I cannot understand, words that merge with the cawing of rooks and the chopping of wood.

He stops talking and, taking off his cap, reaches out as if to embrace the view, then turns to give me a toothless smile. Plucking at the textile of his trousers he sits down among the dandelions, the movement, one of deliberate slowness of a body that knows its limitations. It has endu-red a lifetime of hard work, witnessed by a bent back, by twisted nails and swollen joints, and by deep creases on the back of his neck - they remind me of a spring run-off pattern left behind on a river's shoal of sand.

I peer into his face, exotically marked by a myriad crea-ses radiating from eyes, nose and mouth - where in the west do we see this kind of face? I listen carefully to his voice, to the flow of vowels and consonants, to the sudden hiss of p, s, and z all rolled into one, sharp sound. The sounds I hear belong, they describe the landscape, the river - and his personal history. But their meaning remains a mystery, there is no way of communicating directly, of asking this man about his life, how he sees the landscape after living in it all his life. This barrier between us stresses my isolation from everything essentially Polish - I am a stranger here.

"What one thinks of any region, while traveling through, is the result of at least three things: what one knows, what one imagines and how one is disposed," wrote Barry Holstun Lopez[2]. What did I know about Poland? Next to nothing of its culture, and only mere snippets of a turbulent history of strife and pain. Of its last upheaval, the breakdown of communism initiated and effectuated by Solidarity in the early 80's, I knew a little more. Poland to me, had few more dimensions than its outline on a map.

I imagined a land covered with grey from fumes issued by large, infernally black steelworks. Poland was a coun-try caught in the stranglehold of a stagnant economy, bur-dened by a hopelessly outdated industry, a country with little to offer its people in the way of better prospects for the future. My imagination resembled grainy photo-graphs, with dark shadows and shades of grey.

But now that I have travelled across its vastness, and have had a chance to scrutinize a small, forgotten piece of this second largest country in Europe, I have had to alter the preconceptions which had taken root in my mind.

The reality of Poland

The lack of change and hope in former communist countries is what primarily occupies western press agencies. They document the regression of social developments, the political and economic instability, and the environment is, if at all, presented as the victim of an impending environmental catastrophe. All these the sad result of nearly fifty years of idealistic rule by men who were "promoted according to their party loyalty, not their demonstrated ability."[3]

Many were aware of the damage inflicted on the environment during the communist regime, but it was kept a political secret. Official reports on pollution emissions were swept under the carpet out of fear of damage to the illusion of a communist paradise. Now, after the downfall, it is all in the open.

Polish industries were born in an explosive boom based on five-year booster plans and 1950's technology. Today they can be truly labelled 'infernal' in that they present an imminent health hazard to people working in, or living near industrial centres where pollution control is a virtually non-existent luxury. Here, men and women are exposed to situations that jeopardize their health, their lives - statistics show that about half of the Polish factory workers die before they reach a pensionable age.[4] These areas have been designated as 'ecological catastrophe regions', and there are nearly thirty of them. Home to one third of the 38 million Poles, most are situated near the Czech border in Upper Silesia, and all are heavily polluted - on infra-red photographs taken from space they show up as ugly 'hotspots'. On the ground, levels of pollution are way above the norm for lead, cadmium and other dangerous metals.

Statistics also show that more than fifty per cent of the pollution measured in the country is produced on Polish soil. Sulphuric dioxide and nitrogen oxides emitted from Polish factory chimneys are assimilated by acid rain clouds blown in from all across the industrial belt of Europe, from Czechoslovakia, but also from Germany, Belgium and even from faraway Britain. When it rains, acids rain down onto cities, national monuments, villages and trees, on crops and into fields - wash into the soil, into groundwater, into drinking water reservoirs. Plants react - they die. Trees take longer to die. Humans react too, and though respiratory diseases, cancer, and high infant mortality are accepted as being linked to pollution, scientists hesitate to accept a causal connection. They are quick to point out other contributing factors such as poor housing, unhealthy food, inadequate medical facilities, smoking and abuse of alcohol.

A warm day in a small village in north-eastern Poland. A group of foreign artists, press people, and representatives of various conservation organisations sit about in the

With a clarity that cuts right through the sombre images I know that it is in the east where Europe's heritage of her natural past lies.

In the east, not in the west.

In Poland I looked, and listened, and tried to learn of the hopes and dreams of people who abide by the land; whose future has always been closely tied to the fluctuating rhythm of seasons. What they now face is a future that may change all that. Despite their will, and capabilities, they cannot stop the scales from tipping the wrong way.

I have learned. I feel that the remoteness has diminished between my world and theirs. I find it less easy to shrug off their worries and despair, and the landscape they inhabit now seems to lie at my own doorstep.

2) Wooden cottage and flowering plumtrees. 3) Barnyard geese.
Photography: Fred F. Hazelhoff, unless otherwise stated.

Poland lies in Central Europe, a country with a surface area of approximately 312,000 sq. kms and a population of 38 milion. It is divided into 49 'voivodships' or provinces. The capital Warsaw has nearly 1,8 milion inhabitants.

A large part of the country consists of a low and relatively flat landscape, a part of the European Plain which extends from Northern Germany into Belorussia (White Russia). Mountain ranges are only found in the deep south where the Carpathian Mountains, the High Tatra, with peaks above 2000 metres, and the Sudeten Mountains form a natural boundary with the Czech Republic and Belorussia. Parallel to the foot of the mountains lies a landscape of terraces and hills never exceeding 600 metres. Here, in the uplands of Silezia, Little Poland and Lublin many of the industrial centres are situated.

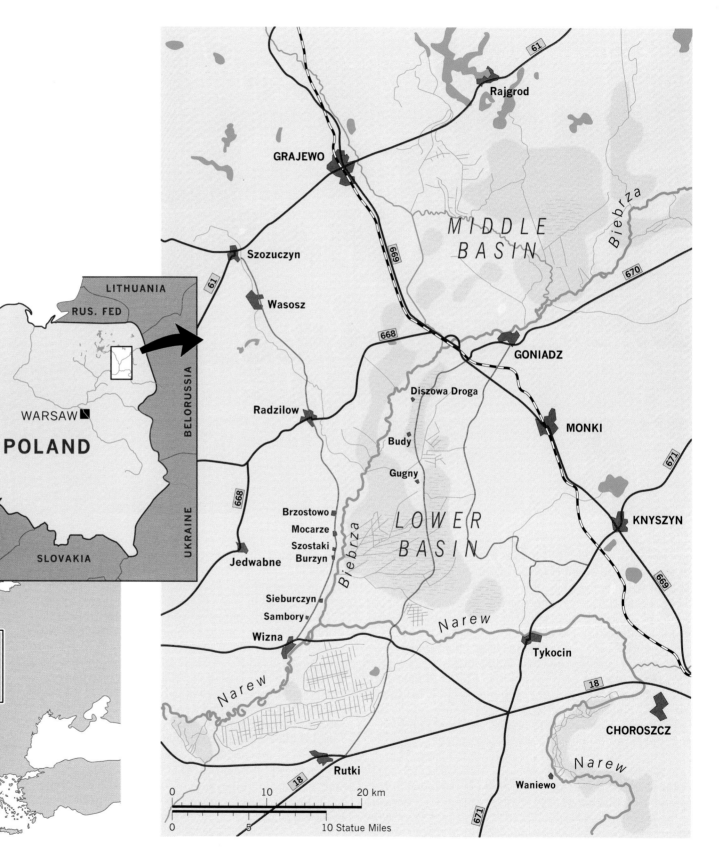

4

5

4) *Biebrza landscape.* 5) *Biebrza transport.*

sun; the artists with an eye turned to the sky for migrating raptors and ears tuned in to Krzysztof Wolfram, spokesman for the 'Green Lungs of Poland' project. He talks about the complex economic plan for developing the northeast of Poland in a 'soft' way that will guarantee its ecological diversity. He shows enthusiasm and great feeling for Poland, and for the problems that beset it. Wolfram: *"Now* is the time to change, the last chance to do things in a different way - but now is a difficult moment to talk about ecological protection in Poland. What the Polish people want *first of all* is a rapid change for the better of their own situation. They are aware that conservation is expensive, and that it restricts certain economic possibilities. On top of that the media are interested in other problems, so general awareness of pollution is very low nowadays. What we need is a change of mentality, and to bring that about a 'scenario of change'. The Green Lungs of Poland plan contains such a scenario. It must be made clear, through international and local conservation

organisations, that it is not profitable to destroy nature. Education is a key factor, we desperately need an education programme to try and raise awareness - but our schooling system is now completely disorganized."

Of all these problems, restructuring the economy has priority over reducing pollution and expensive pollution control in government planning. When the old fashioned, non-profitable industries disappear, which is inevitable, thousands will be out of work. Looming questions confront the Polish government: where do we get the money to keep the economy on its feet, the money to pay for modern industries, for better medical care and social welfare, for more jobs, and for higher wages? And, one can add, what money will be left for cleaning up the country?

"Because pollution was used by political activists as a stick to beat the ruling communists," Jon Thompson wrote in his article "East Europe's Dark Dawn"[5], "and because money and jobs are far more important to the man in the street, the pollution issue will likely fade from the head-

lines. The sewage and sulphur dioxide, however, will still be there. To achieve the standards we all take for granted, huge sums of money will have to be spent. But whose money? How will Eastern Europe's struggling economies pay for these necessary improvements, let alone the clean technologies we are now beginning to expect? Enormous tasks lie ahead. To tackle them, East and West must join together. But will Eastern Europe's new rulers find the environment as important now as they did when they were in the opposition?"

This is the reality of Poland.

It is understandable but unfortunate that journalists are focused on the negative aspects that stand out during the opening up of communist countries, unfortunate that they fail to notice that there is 'gain' as well. Europe gropes towards an understanding of the East, towards some kind of union, but its fear of engaging and burdening itself with the debilitating problems makes it blind to the wealth of pristine landscape, of habitat and wildlife . We in the West, who long ago have exchanged our wilderness for agricultural, industrial and urban development, find it difficult to accept that land and wildlife are an asset to all of Europe.

The extensive Biebrza and Narew marshes are situated only 200 kilometres from Warsaw and less than 500 from the nuclear plant at Chernobyl. How was it possible that a landscape, rich in plant and animal life, survived despite the presence of human settlement along its fringes, despite pollution?

There appears to be one, basic reason: poverty. A lack of money on all levels of society: on goverment level a lack of money for agricultural development, regional administration's lack of money for large scale drainage schemes, a farmer's lack of money to invest in machines, fertilizer and even manpower.

The Biebrza marshes in the northeast of Poland have been left undisturbed for centuries simply because there was little interest in agricultural development, and now there is no money - leaving, temporarily, the largest peat bogs in all of Europe of prime importance from an ecological point of view, undisturbed.

Water is the essence of the living marsh - it affects all life. The unaltered water-table, unpolluted ground and river water, the natural dynamics of river flow and overflow, are important regulating factors for all reaches of plant and animal life.

The extent of flooding varies from year to year, depending on winter downfall and the amount of ice and snow that melts as temperatures rise in early spring. The density of plantlife is high and varied, with flora communities existing in different stages of development close to each other as a result of the zonation of flooding. Insects and fish relying on the natural dynamics of the marsh for propagation, in turn influence mammals and birds.

The variety of birdlife of the Biebrza attracts a growing number of birdwatchers from various European countries. They come to see the great numbers of migrants returning from their wintering grounds in southern Europe, Africa and Asia. Ducks and geese forage on the river and its backwaters, as do several species of grebes. Ruff, black-tailed godwits and other waders make use of the soggy meadows and islands of sedge. The reeds abound with birds such as the stealthy spotted and little crakes, bitterns and warblers. And marsh songbirds including an important part of the European population of the aquatic warbler. A total of 235 different species makes the Biebrza marshes invaluable as an ornithological 'hotspot'.

Scientists have found in the Biebrza an ideal reference area for planned restorations of peatbog ecosystems in their own countries; research is being carried out on all aspects of marsh life by scientists and students from Polish, Dutch and German universities.

This too, is the reality of Poland.

"The Lord giveth, and the Lord taketh away, but he is no longer the only one to do so," wrote Aldo Leopold in his memorable *A Sand County Almanac*.[6] It is an analysis of man's close ties with the land, of the disastrous ways in which he attempts to manage his surroundings. "Man always kills the thing he loves, and so we the pioneers have killed our wilderness. Some say we had to. Be that as it may, I am glad I shall never be young without wild country to be wild in. Of what avail are forty freedoms without a blank spot on the map?"[6]

Since Leopold's days before the Second World War, man has waged a continuing war on marshland. Even as I write there are people out there trying to subdue 'wasteland', render it productive by draining, by filling in, by fertilising and by replanting. A history of time destroyed by developers whose awareness of the land is measured in figures on diagrams, and in annual reports of yield and loss. Profit - at any cost. Those who manage the land are educated people, no doubt, but they haven't learned to think, or are not prepared to do so, along ecological lines. "Education, I fear, is learning to see one thing by going blind to another. One thing most of us have gone blind to is the quality of the marshes."[6]

Will it be possible to check an ingrained tendency to subjugate and cultivate a wilderness beyond recognition? Arguments must be found that prove that the preservation of marshes will benefit people.

To those concerned by the threat to people's health from pollution and by global warming - the hot-house effect of carbon dioxide - the value of bogs, swamps and marshes lies in their capacity to play a part in regulating climate, by acting as reservoirs, storing carbon in decaying plant material on the swamp bottom for thousands of years.

6

7

6-7) *Typical village scenes: well and timber cottage.*

8

8) *Barns.* 9) *Swamp forest.*

THE INFLUENCE OF MAN

"If the marsh itself has the feel of a primeval wilderness," wrote British artist Bruce Pearson, "the rural landscape on either side of the valley has the medieval touch."

Because marshes have never been an attractive area for people, colonization took place rather late, tribes coming in to settle the marshes as late as the Middle Ages. Medieval man kept to the high ground, building settlements on the moraines and scattered smaller dunes - where the villages still are situated.

Dusty roads set off with lattice fences lead to villages almost merging into the landscape and partly hidden by bushes and trees. Fields are only fenced in around the villages, rarely with barbed wire. Workhorses are a common sight on village roads and in fields. A field being ploughed by man and horse, accompanied by rooks gliding through the dust, a horse-drawn cart on the crest of a slope. In the eyes of many visitors these picturesque scenes

belong either in nostalgic paintings or in open-air museums - but here horses are used out of necessity, not romance.

Generally the farms are small, 10 - 15 hectares average, and self supporting. The farmers keep livestock for milk, eggs and meat, grow their own potatoes and vegetables, some cereals like barley and rye, and supplement their diets by - illegal - hunting and fishing. The farms are privately owned as they have been for a long time. Communism, following in the wake of a victorious Red Army in 1944 didn't change so very much for the Polish farmer, since about 90% of the farmers already owned their land.

In the Biebrza region the farmer's life hasn't been as completely invaded by mechanization as it has in more prosperous areas. Only a few of the farms show the messy signs of the machine age: a collection of rusting farming implements, Ursus tractors and oily patches on levelled concrete barnyards. The richer farmers own fields on the high parts of the river embankment, where the ground can support the weight of tractors - small holders working the moist meadows have to rely on horses.

The influence of low-intensity agricultural activity on the landscape is minimal but essential: grazing of domestic animals and annual mowing check the natural growth of vegetation.

In winter the marshes freeze over, giving support to horse drawn carts that are driven deep into the marshes to collect the stacked, dried sedge, winter fodder for the cows and pigs. In May the ruts of the carts can still be seen, extending from the meadows bordering on the river well into the marsh - now they disappear into the floodwater. Unfortunately mowing has dwindled over the last thirty years because farmers lack manpower and because they have found animal fodder in more accessible places closer to the villages.

It was the peasant agriculture which kept part of the dynamics of this unstable landscape in check and unchanged for ages - what we see today is a relic of habitat once found all over Europe. If this human activity ceases it could well overthrow the delicate balance: if mowing stops, the marsh will grow thick with scrub; if agriculture is intensified, more fertilizer will be used, and more phosphates washed into the Biebrza by way of drainage ditches. If tourism is developed, more wells will have to be dug, more water used, more sewage systems and septic tanks - and more pollution that will seep through into ground water.

Krzysztof Wolfram: "In general people living here don't realize the value of the area. Their main problem is the hard life of hard work on soil of poor quality, the back-breaking work in the marshes, the extreme weather

9

conditions and meagre incomes. 'What are wetlands good for?' they ask. They don't see the necessity for extra labour on the marsh, so they must be paid to do this kind of work."

Poland, its social and economic systems, farmer and peasant included, are in a period of transition. Convictions prevailing during communist rule seem less certain, less convincing, now that the future is open. What should a man think? What should he do, what can he do, now that the old ideas and ideals have been proved false?

"In the rush to intensify and modernise farming methods, and to increase efficiency, the destructive mistakes of agri-business will be repeated in these still undisturbed rural wilds of eastern Europe," says Bruce Pearson. "Many of the most valuable wildlife habitats are in danger of being destroyed. But what choices can be offered to poor rural communities that will enable them to continue with agricultural practices which are in harmony with the landscape and will benefit wildlife, and which will enable the people to move away from an unrewarding economic existence on the land?"

Scientists and concerned individuals have acknowledged the bio-diversity and special value of the Biebrza area and some, like Polish photographer Wiktor Wolkow, have dedicated their lives to its beauty and fascinating changeability. Together they have formed 'The Friends of the Biebrza' and their attempts to convince politicians of the value of the marshes have resulted in the establishment in 1989 of the Biebrza Landscape Park, covering 46,000 ha.

It was a first step, and it should be followed by the next: the establishment of The Biebrza National Park - a move at present frustrated through lack of funds.

This book presents the work of painters, illustrators and photographers - men and women with different backgrounds and ideals but sharing a mutual interest and concern for nature.

This book is about what we saw, but also about what we felt and thought. We were inspired by the natural riches, by the animals and by the people that inhabit this landscape. This book is our way of saying: it is worth protecting, and there still is time… but it is running out fast.

ARTISTS FOR NATURE FOUNDATION

It was brave of ARTISTS FOR NATURE FOUNDATION to invite over thirty artists to the northeast of Poland and close to folly to expect them to cover the 90,000 hectares of the *Biebrza* and *Narew* marshes in a fortnight. But what the ANF set out to do was accomplished: artists with widely varying backgrounds worked together to produce a body of work which can be used to draw attention to an area unique in Europe. The Foundation is pleased with the results: more than 2000 sketches, paintings and sculptures were produced during the meeting, from which a selection has been made for this book and the travelling exhibition *'Portrait of a Living Marsh'*.

ARTISTS FOR NATURE FOUNDATION was developed from a meeting of artists on the Dutch barrier island *Schiermonnikoog* in May 1990. There the artists felt that work produced at such gatherings could be used to focus attention on areas which are under threat. That same year the ANF was established in The Netherlands as a charity under Dutch law. The Foundation's aims are to arrange international meetings of artists to portray threatened nature areas all over the world. These meetings are organised in close association with international conservation organizations such as WORLDWIDE FUND FOR NATURE (WWF) and its local branches, and with conservation organisations and experts familiar with local conditions.

By using the artwork for exhibitions and books the ANF wants to help publicise the need for conservation of habitat and the preservation of species under threat, and hopes to influence politicians and authorities to take action.

(For address see 'List of Organisations' on page 190)

10

11) *Denis Clavreul: 'Biebrza landscape' - pencil and watercolour*
29.5 x 41.5 cms.
12) *Bruce Pearson: 'Boatman and terns' - pencil and watercolour 21 x 30 cms.*

13

13) *Hans Geuze: 'Storks on the Biebrza marsh' - watercolour 36 x 53 cms.*
14) *Michael Warren: 'Yellow wagtail and dandelions' - watercolour*
    14 x 12 cms.
15) *John Busby: 'Black terns' - watercolour 19 x 31 cms.*

16

16) *David Daly: 'Ruff' (detail) - watercolour 25 x 35 cms.*
17) *Tomasz Cofta: 'Bluethroat' - gouache 15 x 21 cms.*
18) *Peter Partington: 'Study sheet with birds of the Biebrza: snipe, stork, white-*
    winged black terns, lapwing, redshank, yellow wagtail and aquatic warbler '
    - watercolour 29 x 40.5 cms.

20

19) *Robert Bateman: 'Biebrza wetland' - acrylic on board 61 x 91 cms.*
20) *Robert Bateman: 'Farms overlooking the Biebrza Valley' - acrylic on board
16 x 30 cms.*

21

22

24

23

21) *Robert Greenhalf: 'Ploughing horse' - handcoloured etching 23 x 25 cms.*
22) *Denis Clavreul: 'Well' (detail) - pencil 31 x 40 cms.*
23) *Charles Donker: 'Old shed' - watercolour 28 x 38 cms.*

Victoria Crowe

27

26

24) *Kim Atkinson: 'Cows and godwits' - mixed media 52 x 134 cms.*
25) *Victoria Crowe: 'Decorated crucifix, Waniewo' - watercolour 32 x 24 cms.*
26) *Jon Fjeldså: 'Reedbuntings among the reeds' - watercolour 31 x 35 cms.*
27) *Bruce Pearson: 'Montague's harrier hunting close to a village' - mixed
     media 37 x 45 cms.*

29

28) *Victoria Crowe: 'Bogbean' - watercolour 32 x 24 cms.*

29) *Ad Cameron: 'Well and jackdaw' - pen and watercolour 30 x 24 cms.*
   - Dutch illustrator Ad Cameron expresses his sadness at the loss of
   nature: "It is a gradual process; you can compare it to a cake: first a
   small piece is taken, then, another small piece, and another and so
   on - and then the cake is gone. People are like mice, they gnaw and
   gnaw - until nothing is left. Then they complain."

30) *John Busby: 'Biebrza landscape' - watercolour 25 x 34.5 cms.*

32

31) *Darren Rees: 'Montague's harrier over farmland' - watercolour*
   39 x 57 cms.
32) *Peter Partington: 'Biebrza landscape' - watercolour 26 x 38.5 cms.*
33) *Chris Rose: 'Black-tailed godwit' - watercolour 21 x 29 cms.*

33

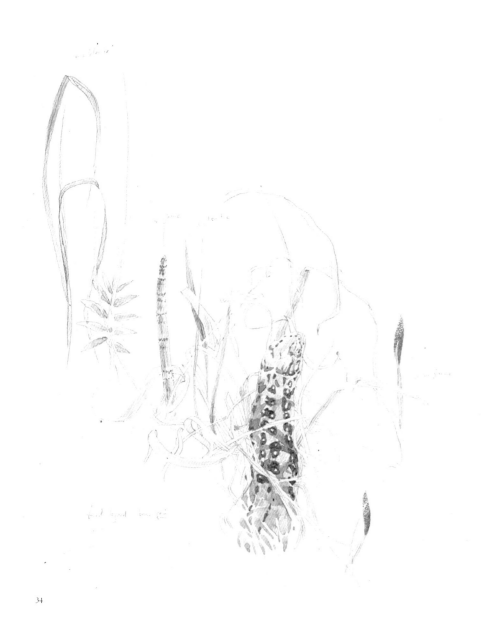

34) *Denis Clavreul: 'Lizard on the marsh' (detail) - pencil and watercolour*
   31 x 40 cms.
35) *Vadim Gorbatov: 'Elk, Biebrza valley' - watercolour 30 x 43 cms.*

35

A FARMER'S WORLD

"My only regret about the trip is that the language barrier prevented me from asking the people what it is really like living in a community like Waniewo at present, what it was like in the past, and what their fears and expectations for the future."
- Robert Greenhalf (England)

Leaving the mix of fast cars, horse drawn carts and lumbering trucks on the main road between Warsaw and Bialystok our bus takes a road that winds southwards through arable lands dotted with small woods, past freshly ploughed fields and fields lined with tender shoots of barley and rye, and through Barbizon-like villages where roofs carry bulky nests adorned with storks, the shape of each nest echoed in a whitish halo of droppings.

Looking down into farmyards where cockerels strut among feeding chickens, where playing children mingle with ducks and playful piglets, a rich mixture of sights, sounds and smells is presented. In one of the villages a Communion is in full progress beneath a colourfully decorated roadside statue of the Holy Virgin and as we rumble past, a kneeling child peers at us from the corner of one eye.

"A familiar déjà vu of cabbage soup, bright patterns, fretwork and wrought iron, decorated country shrines, mud roads and wooden houses," said Victoria Crowe, who had travelled to Russia during her student days. Dutch artist Charles Donker remarked: "Some of the villages we came through remind me very much of early Chagall paintings, especially those in which he visualized his memories of Witebsk and western Russia."

A dead rook, strung up above the rye, catches the wind and flutters paper-like around its stake. The tight lane of tall poplars bordering the road suddenly opens up to a large crucifix, its shape rigid and scrawny as a scarecrow among the gracefully swaying branches and their new-green leaves. At the crossroads we pass an effigy of the Holy Virgin, hands clasped in eternal lamentation - abruptly the sound of the tires changes as they encounter the uneven cobblestones, and those slumbering are shaken awake.

We have reached Waniewo, a small settlement on the edge of the river Narew. A village of not more than forty farms, most of them simple, wooden structures, only occasionally interspersed with larger buildings made of brick, all laid out before the stern gaze of yet another Holy Virgin placed halfway up the single tower of the church.

Victoria Crowe, (from her sketchbook): "Extraordinary farm buildings, a shed for the pigs, one for three cows, one for the horse, one huge all-purpose barn deep in straw, complete with laying hens. A space for recycling waste - compost. I think beet leaves, weighted down and packed flat, looking like tobacco. Wood carefully sorted into bundles of small, medium and larger circumferences. A little place for joinery, a cart, and all one family's needs. Amazing village surrounded by huge reed beds, not many recognisable plants apart from bulrush, maces, pollarded willow, some tiny waterplants, mint, cuckoo flower and water bitter cress."

In early morning the sounds that prevail are those of a farmer's world: the rattle of buckets, a crowing rooster and clattering hooves in a barnyard, short, sharp commands as the frisky horse is harnessed to its cart. A wooden gate squeaks on its hinges.

After they have been milked, the cows are led with jangling chains to the meadows where each animal is staked down singly on the verge of the tussocky marsh.

The men take the fresh milk to the coöp building near the crossroads in the centre of the village. They file down the road with milk canisters dangling from bicycles, or ranked on wooden carts that creak but roll softly on worn rubber tires. The smell of burning cigarettes lingers in the air.

In front of the little white building, opposite the village well, there is a pile-up of carts, horses and men. Shortlegged dogs scamper among the legs and wheels. The men move slowly in and out of the gloom of the interior where clear vodka bottles and small glasses reflect little pinpricks of light. One of them barks something at me, others laugh. Vodka loosens the blood, and the tongue - even at this early hour.

Walking past the farmyards I hear pigs squealing in their pens; hens scratch around the large, decorated barn doors. By the time the sun is up the roosters are all through their crowing; one, jerking his frilled head, keeps a glinting eye on his hens while leading them across the road and into the lush field.

37

36) *Aerial view of Waniewo. Photo: Wiktor Wolkow.*
37) *At the Waniewo coöp building early in the morning.*

38

39) *Cart horse and foal.*

Children, scrubbed clean and carefully combed, cycle off to school while within the barnyards the daily chores continue: the animals are tended to, scarved women carry buckets of kitchen refuse to the pigs and return to their kitchens with an apronful of eggs. An old woman hauls wearily on the long see-saw lever to raise water from the well and behind her a bowlegged farmer carries a manure-laden pitchfork to the midden; he grins and nods his head at me.

"The greenhouses made of yards of white plastic look like UFO's when the morning sunbeams shine through them," says Else Behring. "The cold, clean air makes me shudder as I take deep breaths, a luxury I rarely enjoy in Copenhagen. The meadow is freckled yellow with dandelions, jackdaws are flapping their wings, they tease the calves! I gaze and gaze, my childhood on a farm dancing through my mind - a paradise I have lost."

John Busby: "The people seem very competent at everything they do. They work hard and long hours but they do not rush, the pace is sustainable. There is little waste - milk drums are mended with soldering irons and hammer.

They are adept at all uses of wood, most practical problems can be solved. It would seem to be the political and outside economic issues which are unsolvable, and who knows what the pressure to become more modern will bring. To me the advanced farms looked untidier than the poorer ones where everything was well made, and with pride, it seemed."

In a small field alongside their house, an elderly couple work their way up the furrows on their knees, pulling out weeds. When I return after a day's painting in the Biebrza valley, elated from the sheer vastness of the landscape, they are still at work, still on their knees. The shadow of an overhead stork slides down a barn wall, sweeps across the furrows and the rounded backs of the man and woman before converging again with the bird at the far end of the field. There the stork finds a clump of dry weeds, snatches it up and dances excitedly with flapping wings. The old couple do not notice, they are focused on a world no bigger than the few square feet of earth directly in front of them.

39

In the long, low greenhouses temperatures have been building up all day; looking in through an open door I feel the press of the damp, stifling air. Inside, man follows horse. Harrowing the soil, they go round and round as if caught in a maze, eyes turned downwards, and inwards. For the moment their world is sixty paces down, twelve across, sixty paces up and twelve across.

Two dusty men sip their Czech beers on the steps of the village shop - hardly recognizable as such - and stare after Larry McQueen, as he walks down the road towards the church. He is dressed in blue, wears a white cap and is covered with the paraphernalia of an American wildlife painter: binoculars, camera and lenses, telescope and tripod, and all his sketching materials in a pack. A tractor revs up, and pulling a cartload of men rattles past, hiding all in a cloud of diesel fumes and dust. An immaculate Madonna, an omnipresent symbol of the surge of old desires and new ideals in Poland, seems to hang above the dust.

Lawrence McQueen: "The importance of the church in setting the daily rhythm in the village soon became apparent to me. Here was devotion early each morning and every evening; twice daily we could hear beautiful singing from our borrowed house next to the church. Its architecture dominated the horizon from the fields and marsh surrounding the village. I could even hear music from the church while studying aquatic warblers in the marsh."

Victoria Crowe: "The church is much in evidence here, bells ringing at 6.30 a.m. and for midday Angelus. Daily morning and evening services. So the liturgical year must be another regulating factor to everyday life - a direct parallel to the movement and cycle of animal life."

At face value harmony exists between farmers and landscape, in what to us seemed a Polish pastoral. But behind barriers we rarely penetrated lay worry and frustration, and anger directed at only partly understood changes in the farmer's universe. Agriculture has lost its importance as an economic certainty in Poland, and with it reasons for investing in machines, fertilizers, pesticides and drainage of marshland. The farms stay small and primitive, making it difficult, if not impossible, for farmers to get better yields, let alone profit.

The younger generation doesn't want to lead such a hard and uncertain life, villages depopulate, people move to the cities or abroad. Only recently the outflow has been checked - because there is nowhere else to go.

"It looks like an idyll," says Dutch artist Siegfried Woldhek, "but people don't lead rich lives… Seeing them toil, I wonder how long this will last. It is inconceivable that it will, because their way of cultivating the land is so backward when seen in a European context. As soon as money begins to flow into Poland people will either leave, or they will want to do things on a larger scale. In both cases the landscape will be affected, and what could happen is what has happened all over Europe: within the next twenty years all will be destroyed. And people will say: we never expected this would happen…"

Else Behring: "In search of new models, I stop in front of a small house where a chicken is tethered by a string around one leg. She is surrounded by tiny chicks. The family sitting on the steps smile when I sit down on the grass to draw. The grandad totters on his stiff legs, 'cheep,cheep,cheep' he says and sprinkles a little meal. He feeds them often, just to keep them near me. The light fades, and he brings out a cardboard box, places the hen in it and all the chicks jump into his hands. He nods goodbye and carries the little balls of down into security for the night."

40) *At the well.*

Darkness seems to grow from the earth, it swallows the villages, and when the lights go out behind the shutters, houses and barns merge with trees, become part of the landscape - except for the Madonna of Waniewo church, she floats in a circle of light, held aloft by a halo of electric lightbulbs.

The sounds of the marsh wash over the houses and barns, over the punts lying still in the shallows, over the cobbled roads and fields, and over the stork that sleeps on the lamp-post across the mayor's house. From somewhere high up in a sky so bright with starlight it seems unreal to my city eyes, a nightjar chatters.

A walk through the village at this ungodly hour causes pandemonium to break loose among the village dogs, they bark and growl, invisible behind invisible fences. I leave the village and walk down the road to an abandoned house; its thatched roof punctured by a tree, the garden an overgrown mass of brambles that hide the hollow carcass of a dog stretched out under a shelter. Windows reflect the sky and the gentle movement of trees. There is a delicate fragrance of poplars in the air. A roe deer barks, probably hidden in the black band of trees. Against their blackness shimmer limp white sheets of plastic, tied to posts to ward off wild boar, marking the boundary of a barley field. There, I saw lapwings chase a coursing harrier on a day full of colour.

Something rustles in the vegetation, but there is nothing to be seen. Do lapwings move around the field at night, or do they sit tight, while covering their young with warm, dry down? I hold my breath and listen, but whatever was there has caught my scent and fled.

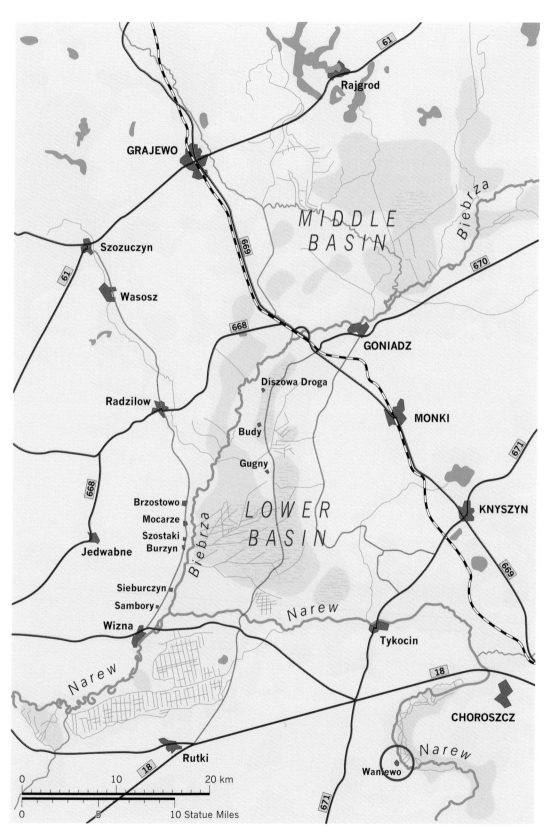

Waniewo

Waniewo *(150 inhabitants)* was first mentioned in a 1447 document; in it reference was made of a bridge, the link between the region of Mazowsze and Lithuania in the north. The village boasted a castle which was destroyed early in the 16th century, a result of a bloody feud between the Radziwill and Gasztold families.

Waniewo became 'somewhere in nowhere' by the end of the 16th century, its church the only feature distinguishing it from surrounding hamlets. The present church was built in the 19th century.

Waniewo suffered heavily during both world wars, coming under fire in 1915 and in 1944. It was rebuilt after 1945 in the traditional way, using timber and thatch. The village even prospered in the late 1960's and early 1970's; with many villagers beginning to specialize in vegetable products for the Bialystok market.

It was at this time that the more prosperous farmers replaced their wooden houses with houses made of brick and concrete.

Unfortunately a recent administration system reform has cut off the village from the markets of Bialystok, forcing the farmers to look for new markets to sell their products.

41

41) *Peter Partington: 'Biebrza Village' - watercolour 29 x 41.5 cms.*

42

42) *Michael Warren: 'Ortolan bunting near Waniewo' - watercolour 38.5 x 21 cms.*
43) *Robert Bateman: 'Waniewo cemetery' - acrylic on paper 11 x 28.5 cms.*
    - In the 18th century, under Prussian rule, cemeteries were moved to the outskirts of villages and towns for reasons of hygiene. But now the village has expanded, extending beyond its former boundaries and surrounding the cemetery on three sides.
44) *Robert Bateman: 'Potato basket' - acrylic on paper 23 x 30 cms.*

43

Robert Bateman 1992 ©

44

45

45) *Lawrence B. McQueen: 'Waniewo church' - watercolour 31 x 51 cms.*
- "Late one afternoon I was struck by the shadowy back of the church, looming over the sun-swept fields. The back-lighting enhanced the contortions of orchard trees and gave the scene a Van Gogh-like expression, further symbolizing to me the struggles of survival on this land."

46) *Victoria Crowe: 'Wooden house, Plutycze' - watercolour 25 x 35 cms.*
- "…a Russian Orthodox village; lots of homesteads built along a straight main road. The majority are wooden houses which have a central tiled stone oven, each room incorporating an exposed part of the stone. Inside one house: hand-stencilled decoration over just about every wall and door and even over the glass in the doors. I told the woman how good it looked and asked if she'd done it herself. Tomasz Cofta was there to translate. She seemed apologetic in saying 'yes, we can't afford wallpaper.' If only she could see the endless trendy articles on home-stencilling in Home and Gardens , etc!"

46

"Working in the studio is usually such a solitary experience so I enjoyed being with a group of artists very much, as I did the passing round of sketchbooks and interest in each other's work. My own interests and activities lay outside the majority interest, many in the group could draw moving birds and suggest soft colours and feathers - like dreams. Once I accepted that a weathered barn door with a stack of potatoes in the sunlight was, in essence, just as 'Biebrzan' as a shrike's nest near that long, straight, endless road I felt happy with my researches.

The longer I stayed there, the more everything seemed to get together, and I could begin to feel what was important for me to do. I think my work was divided between the objective plant studies - which I found challenging and satisfying - and the work closely related to the peasant way of life. This simple way of life has enabled the habitat to remain; history's fluctuating borders, and peasant economy, which is non-exploitive, have also helped preserve these areas.

Apart from the ideas of plant species in habitat, the most stimulating event was the peasant women at Sieburczyn. I was able to draw one of them, make colour notes about the pattern and texture of her assorted layers of scarf, jumper, skirt, stockings and huge black rubber galoshes.

Towards the second week I felt I knew what I was doing here, but by the end I had suddenly seen another huge vista of 'things to do' and felt I had left many things undone."

- Victoria Crowe (Scotland)

47) *Victoria Crowe: 'Wooden house, Waniewo' - watercolour 25 x 35 cms.*

48) *Victoria Crowe: 'Zofia inside her house' - watercolour and pastel 25 x 35 cms.*

- "I've become fascinated by Zofia's house and the way she orders her time, the simplicity of her house - one cup, one plate on the kitchen draining board. I think it's the purposefulness and order of her daily life, maybe it is the rigour and grind of poverty, but there is a sense of pride and achievement. I would love to go inside but Eugeniusz[7] says that she would not understand. Today I decided to move away as she looks back at me now and sharply draws her room curtain, so that is a clear enough message.

Throughout all the drawing in the farmyard and fields, observing Zofia's solitary and ordered existence, an understanding of the larger questions, of co-existence, non-exploitation of resource, hard work but to a seasonal rhythm, in tune with nature and with a kind of fulfilment and order, seemed to be revealing itself. I didn't get that feeling of desolate poverty like at home sometimes, where despair is so evident in the filth, rubbish and disorder."

A FARMER'S WORLD

49

50

49) *Denis Clavreul: 'Working in the garden' - watercolour 30 x 41 cms.*
50) *Bruce Pearson: 'Studies of Zofia at work' - pencil and watercolour 37 x 60 cms.*
51) *Keith Brockie: 'Ola, the Sokol cart horse' - watercolour 38 x 56 cms.*
   - "My initial intention was to record the working horse harness. I had to work quickly to delineate the drawing as accurately as possible before the horse became too bored. Even though restrained the horse moved about more than I expected, I constantly had to change position with the horse. Intense artistic concentration from close proximity like this tends to unnerve animals after a while, even pets become uncomfortable in such situations."

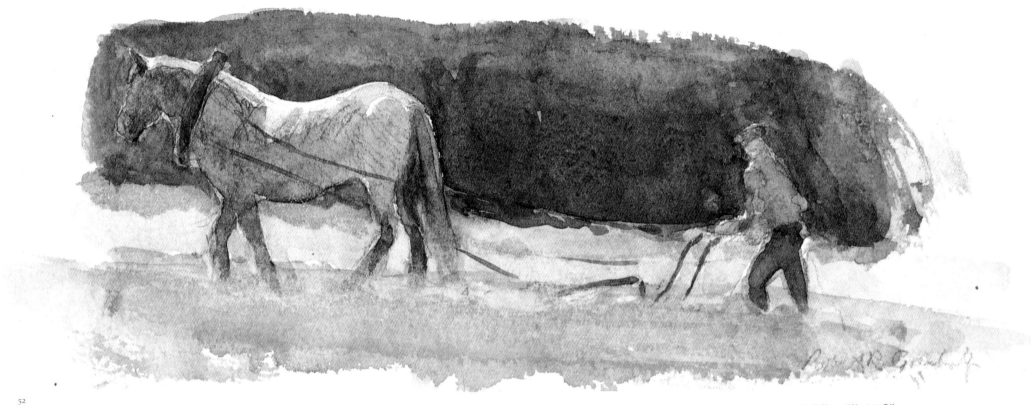

52

53

"It is difficult to sum up my experiences in Poland. I feel I learned a lot, I was enriched both as an artist and person. I hardly prepared myself for this trip because I wanted to be fresh in my approach - to look at things like a child does. There were so many things to marvel at, so much I wanted to draw, I decided against restricting myself to only a few subjects.

Thinking back, the first images that come to mind are of village life, and not wildlife - I suppose because as an artist I have been interested for a long time in the relationship between man and nature. In Poland I was captivated by the contrast between village life and the wilderness with its wide open spaces. I don't think it would be right to idealise the inhabitants of these villages as people who have managed to preserve the virgin landscape by keeping their lives simple - I am pretty sure it was rather a case of enduring their fate than planning ahead in consideration of that 'paradise'.

The warm welcome and smiles of the folks who lodged and fed us were a tacit but effective connection between us artists and villagers. The contact with them during our exhibition in The Barn, as well as that with Polish scientists and artists, was essential to me. I find that difficult to explain, maybe I felt apologetic about the fact that as an artist from the West I could afford the luxury of visiting their country."

- Denis Clavreul (France)

54

52) Robert Greenhalf: 'Plough horses' - watercolour 30 x 22.5 cms.
   - "I was impressed by the toughness of the farmers here, who worked in the fields in the full heat of the day when I was cowering under a tree."
53) Robin D'Arcy Shillcock: 'Firewood' - pen and ink 14 x 19 cms.
54) Denis Clavreul: 'Ploughing the land' - pencil and watercolour 30 x 41 cms.
   - "The atmosphere in the villages reminded me of my childhood visits to my uncles' farms, with all the animals, the sounds and the smells. Without knowing why I was greatly excited by the presence of all the horses."

55

57

Eric Bering

58

John Busby Warriors May 92

56

54

59

55) *Kim Atkinson: 'Ola, In the Sokol Farmyard' - woodcut 75 x 180 cms.*
   - "I realised after I'd printed it that I'd forgotten to reverse the whole
   thing! Now I can't decide whether it is OK or if I will have to cut the
   whole thing again. It is a big sheet of plywood and very awkward in
   the house - I cut it outdoors. Of course it's a different picture, left to
   right round about."
56) *John Busby: 'Hens' - watercolour 12 x 22 cms.*
57) *Else Behring: 'Hens' - pen and ink 20 x 27 cms.*
58) *Else Behring: 'Pigs in sty' - marker drawing 21 x 29 cms.*
59) *Dag Peterson: 'Daylight barnowl' - acrylic 38 x 57 cms.*
60) *Robin D'Arcy Shillcock: 'Waniewo chickens' - oil on board 24 x 30 cms.*

60

61

62

61) *Robin D'Arcy Shillcock: 'On the edge of Narew marsh' - pencil 29 x 42 cms.*

62) *Robert Greenhalf: 'Barnyard fowl' - watercolour 23 x 30 cms.*
    - "The cockerel would strut around, inspecting me with his malevolent eye. It was impossible to read what was in his mind and I half expected his pent-up macho aggression to explode in my direction - but it never did. Instead, one of his long-suffering hens would receive the shock. His seduction technique was devious in the extreme: he would scratch enthusiastically in some corner, uttering sqeaks of delight at some morsel he had supposedly unearthed. This never failed to bring two or three hens running to investigate, whereupon he would unceremoniously jump on the bird of his choice as she bent to look for the food!"

63) *Ad Cameron: 'Dandelion study' - watercolour 30 x 24 cms.*

64) *Piet Eggen: 'Waniewo meadows' - oil 40 x 50 cms.*
    - "I was struck by the flowering dandelion growth that covered fields and pastures and turned them into fields of intense yellow. To the left Waniewo can be seen, on the right the marshes of the Narew begin immediately behind the fence."

64

63

65

66

65) *Lawrence McQueen: 'Dandelions' - watercolour 36 x 25 cms.*
- "I came to realize that the dandelion was a very important compo-
nent of the landscape. At the beginning we saw the budding and
opening, then enlargement and burgeoning of the flower heads.
These created lakes of color, piling up the borders of walkways, buildings, hedges and haystacks with waves of gold.
During our last days, the silver halos of seed heads were everywhere. I saw dandelions as I had never seen them: as truly stunning
wildflowers making gold in spring, instead of as weeds in the
garden.
The dandelions of the Biebrza are made of the brightest, purest yellows I have ever seen. A flower head is not one, but several yellows
concentrically arranged. How could I *not* paint them, but then how
could I not fail? Pigments of paint cannot capture such purity."

66) *Robert Greenhalf: 'Ducks and Daisies' - hand coloured drypoint*
17 x 15 cms.

67) *John Busby: 'Geranium and storks, Waniewo' - watercolour 20 x 38 cms.*

Storks

The white stork became a symbol of the area for the group of foreign artists. "Seeing that great big stork nest on the barn roof and the content birds on top of it was a wonderful experience for me," Swedish artist Dag Peterson said.

In the 1950's there were about 15 - 20 pairs nesting in Waniewo, but in 1962 a big fire laid a great number of old cottages in ashes, and only five nests remained. Of these three have been occupied the past few years. In 1992, the year of the *Artists for Nature Foundation* meeting, only the pair on mayor Sokol's barn bred with success.

Near the church an old barn had recently gone down taking the stork nest with it, so the villagers erected a pole with a platform and a relatively young pair of storks proceded to build a nest - compared to the size of the birds the nest seemed ridiculously small. All the while the storks flew up and down from their artificial nest on the pole, adding sticks and branches, and dropping more than they added to its bulk.

According to the villagers the numbers of storks have dwindled over the past twenty years. The number of nests in one Biebrza village dwindled from forty to ten. Scientists believe this could be more a case of relocation, because population numbers of storks in eastern Poland are fairly consistent. But there is a marked decline of storks in the west of Poland, as there is all over Western Europe.

67

68) *Kim Atkinson: 'Stork' - charcoal and watercolour 56 x 75 cms.*

69) *Dag Peterson: 'The next door neighbours, tree sparrows at stork's nest' -*
   acrylic 36 x 52 cms.

70) *Lawrence McQueen: 'Mating storks' - watercolour 15 x 23 cms.*

71) *Andrew Haslen: 'Stork' - pencil and watercolour 23 x 18 cms.*

70

71

72

White Stork —
Warmiewo.

73

White Storg —
Bworush.

74

72) *Andrew Haslen: 'Storks' - pencil and watercolour 57 x 77 cms.*
73-74) *Michael Warren: 'Studies from sketchbook' - coloured pencil 20 x 14 cms.*

75

75) *Robert Bateman: 'Stork on nest' - acrylic on board 15 x 21 cms.*

76) *Darren Rees: 'Stork I' - watercolour 18 x 24 cms.*
   - "I spent two days painting storks at the nest near Waniewo church; this drew the attention of several villagers, both young and old. The children were most communicative, they were totally uninhibited, looking through my telescope and binoculars and teaching me Polish. On another occasion I was painting two storks in the dusk. A child joined me as I unpacked paints, palette and paper and watched the whole process from blank sheet to finished watercolour, some 45 minutes."

77) *Michael Warren: 'White Stork, Waniewo' - watercolour 18 x 25 cms.*
   - "This stork frequented fields around the church to feed and collect sticks and other material for its nest. I saw it fly with a large stick momentarily framed within the shape of the church building. I recall being very cold while working on this picture."

76

77

16.5.92

79

78

78) Darren Rees: 'Stork II' - watercolour 18 x 24 cms.
79) Chris Rose: 'Stork portrait' - watercolour 14 x 18 cms.
80) Robert Greenhalf: 'Storks,Waniewo' - watercolour 25.5 x 33 cms.
- "A memorable after-dinner session, sitting near the church, painting the storks on their artificial nest pole. Both birds were at the nest, preening and dozing. A real gift. They were backlit from the low evening sun, but through the telescope they were more than silhouettes. Preening finished they flapped lazily down to the fields a hundred yards away, here they paused to rearrange their plumage on the brow of a hill, against a backdrop of haystacks and distant woods, before stalking sedately down the slope and out of sight. The damp evening air gave a soft feel to the painting and it did not dry till I got back to camp."

A FARMER'S WORLD

WILDLIFE OF THE NAREW

"Long, crooked shadows fell over the river and muffled sounds crept along the murky banks. In the creaking of the thick beech branches, in the rustling of the willows trailing their leaves in the water, I heard the utterances of the mysterious beings of whom Olga had spoken.
- Jerzy Koszinski[8]

"Dawn is half an hour away, but there is a pale light across the marsh, enough to check for paddles and to load up my sketching bits and pieces," writes Bruce Pearson in a reminiscence of his visit to the Narew marsh. "The night has brought a heavy dew and a mist which clings to the marsh, allowing only willow tops and tall reed heads to show in the first wash of morning colour."

"With the deep resonance of hidden fog-horns, the booming of bitterns echoes through the marsh like a sudden rush of wind over the top of a huge and empty jug. The sound is hard to pin-point, but there must be two or three birds calling. In the tangle of willows close by a lesser whitethroat is singing and thrush nightingales, bluethroats and a golden oriole are distinctive in the growing chorus as I push myself out into the channel and turn upstream towards the Narew."

"The web of channels are cut by villagers all along the margins for ease of travel, fishing and easy access to houses strung out along the bank. Villagers must know these watery byways intimately, but gliding through the reed-clogged maze there are few reference points to guide a stranger reliably. A muffled voice or cockerel calling in the village helps confirm the general direction, while I try to remember the route I was taken by guide yesterday morning."

"Further out in the marsh the channels are wider and the flow stronger, with swirling patches of open water and banks lined with thick vegetation. I turn the canoe into a tight channel, and gliding out of the other end surprise an otter on the far bank. It turns suddenly and almost without sound slips into the water and is gone."

"With the bow of the canoe pushed into the reeds to keep from drifting I sit making notes and sketches of the otter - the one animal I wanted to see."

Every time the upper reach of the Narew river floods, floodwater forms a new maze of arms, small lakes and islands of sedges and reeds. Tourist brochures call this part of the river the 'wodna Arcadia', the Polish Amazon, an understandable comparison when looking at aerial photographs: the hundred square kilometres of marsh has a distinct amazonian look.

From a boat the view is more restricted - a world without recognisable landmarks, to the uninitiated a place of many secrets. Men from villages such as Waniewo, Kruszewo, Radule and Panki use the scattered groups of alder and willow as landmarks when they go out to set their nets, or when they take out birdwatchers to see birds in the marsh. Unerringly the boatmen follow the succession of narrow channels, cross open water to disappear into walls of tall sedge and reeds that block all sense of space.

82

81) *Empty hayrick on Narew marsh.*
82) *Photo: Wiktor Wolkow.*

83

83) *Last year's reeds, Narew marsh.* 84) *Punt, Narew marsh.*

There are numerous backwaters with little or no current where water lilies cover the surface, and in places the wind cannot reach extensive beds of watersoldier thrive. Their cockades of pointed, serrated leaves breaking the water's surface are favoured as nesting sites by black terns.

Some channels are impenetrable because they are covered with floating vegetation; across the water's surface the riverbanks grow towards each other in a closely knit mat of the remains of reeds, infested by sedge and other marsh plants.

The habitat of dark water and plants anchored by rhizomes to a murky peat bottom form an essential environment for insect and fish life. Some fish, like tench, bream and crucian carp spawn and feed on an abundance of insects, worms, leeches and watersnails in the peat layer.

The otter - which thrives on fish - abounds, as does another aquatic mammal, the beaver. Both are difficult to observe, but occasionally beaver lodges can be seen, heavy mounds of packed mud and branches in contrast to

the airy motion of reeds. An encounter with the largest of wild mammals, the elk, comes as a memorable surprise. Elk look too heavy for such a fragile environment. The encounter is so unexpected that the shape of its huge ears, its hollow back and its delicate looking legs are retained as a kind of afterimage on the retina, long after the animal has disappeared - with incomprehensible stealth.

Bitterns stalk furtively among the reeds, holding on to stalks with their oversized, spidery toes. The birds move subtly with the movement of the reeds, blending in so perfectly they become invisible.

All these animals need the marsh, depend on it for food and nesting sites, or for the isolation and cover it offers.

Chris Rose: "The utter peace and tranquility of the marsh in thick mist was unforgettable, and gave this place a timeless quality. Two white-winged black terns silently appeared through the mist with their unmistakeable buoyant flight, disappearing as quickly as they had come. As a pale yellow sun began to part the mist the marsh

84

suddenly seemed terribly fragile, as if by removing the veil this tranquil corner of the world would disappear. At that moment I felt a sense of foreboding, a worry that to bring this place to the world's attention might destroy it. Later it became clear to me that the marsh was not just a place of beauty, rich in wildlife, but that it was a place of work for the villagers."

The boat trips bring reminders of human presence to light: nets strung across narrow channels, bow-nets and crayfish traps hanging from poles just below the water's surface. A single haystack where none is expected. In a narrow 'alley' of reeds an old punt is shoved deep into the reeds, its bright colour flaking - like scales dropping off a dead fish. The reed-mace towering above the rotting boat is suddenly attacked by a pair of blue tits, they rip the light fluff from the dark brown cigar and are gone within seconds, leaving a little fluff to drift down to the surface of the water.

Large tracts of the Narew have been affected by extensive draining which took place in the early 1980's, and according to the North-Podlasie Society for Bird Protection (PTOP) a dozen smaller drainage projects are still being conducted. The drainage has resulted in the loss of more than 50 kilometres of river habitat and was especially disastrous between Rzedziany and the point where Biebrza and narew join.

Przemyslaw Bielicki of PTOP: "Many river islands were laid dry in the late 60's and put to agricultural use. In regulating the flow of water the area's hydrological system was disturbed: water was transported much faster from the valley, causing the marsh to dry out and waterbirds to decline in alarming numbers due to the loss of habitat and food. Nature died!

"The Narew was overshadowed by her smaller 'sister' the Biebrza for a long time. In the years that the Biebrza Valley became internationally known, conferences and seminars were organised and scientists began their research, the landscape of the Narew was being 'improved'. There were no private conservation bodies in those days and the few ecologists who understood the damage had no power to stop the soil reclamation programmes thought up by bureaucrats.

"The only reason why a part of the natural marsh habitat still survives is because of the economical crisis in Poland of the 80's. During that period the importance of the Narew was finally acknowledged, which resulted in the establishment in 1985 of the Narwianski Park - the Narew Landscape Park.

"Unfortunately that is all the state wanted to do for the Narew. We know that to save this marsh 'paper protection' is not enough. The destroyed areas should be restored, re-naturalised, but this idea is totally new to the appointed nature wardens, who have become used to the idea that their concern ends when 'reserve' is stamped across a map.

85

"The situation looks much better now than it did twenty years ago - nowadays there are more conservation organizations and they voice their concern about the Narew marshes. Their initiatives and the fact that the Narew is becoming known abroad will hopefully bring results - although I foresee many bureaucratic hurdles which we will have to take."

While painting the marsh landscape in its early morning beauty on one of the first warm days of our visit, I noticed a sudden burst of hyper-active yellow wagtails all around. They suddenly come through in great numbers, dotting reeds, trees and haystacks, taking insects that rise from between reeds and sedge as temperatures rise. I find myself removing lace-winged flies from wet paint, and from the corner of my eyes watch a sleek female red-backed shrike catch them in mid-air. She uses a nearby strand of rusty wire for a perch, balancing on it with outstretched toes. Her round head bobs and moves in all directions, the

86) *Boatman and punts. Photo: Ysbrand Brouwers.*

Walking in a landscape lit by a full moon is like walking in your own dream. Shapes are painted pure black. Jagged shadows of trees snake away across pastures that reflect the moonlight. The ground seems to come up to your foot every time you take a step, or is your foot plunging into the ground? The cry of a barn owl stops you in your tracks - it once struck terror into the hearts of night travellers, but your anxiety has less to do with that ancestral feeling than with a fear of not seeing the ephemeral shape glide among the barn roofs. But you stay where you are, feeling you have become part of the field. You listen to the cacophony of marsh birds, to the grunts of copulating hedgehogs nearby. As the stars fade the barn owl calls again, once.

In the fragile light of early dawn a man appears from the marsh, strides across the tussocks of sedge without looking down. One can tell at a glance that he knows the marsh, knows it intimately. What has he been doing? What does the marsh mean to someone living on its borders?

Eugeniusz Sokol has lived on and around the marsh all his life. He talks slowly, thoughtfully, has a slow-motion way of moving as if balancing on a punt all the time. "Throughout my life the marsh has meant different things to me," he says. "I was born here, I grew up here, here I am at home. When still a child I worked with my parents in the marshes, we cut the grass and made hay, laying it on ricks, and later, when the marsh was covered by ice we collected the hay for our animals. The marsh meant hard work in those days."

"Later I liked going into the marsh with my friends to fish, even though fishing was forbidden. By selling the fish we had caught we earned a little pocketmoney."

"Nowadays I often go into the marsh alone, to look at animals. I feel in harmony with my surroundings then. The silence, the absence of noise from civilization and the direct contact with nature give me inner peace. Sometimes I return to the same spot over and over, discovering something new each time."

"This river has a life of its own, I feel a certain rhythm. It is big and independent and it will never let itself be forced into the narrow reality of a canal. When I am on the river I feel at peace with myself and - this is very important for me - free."

"For decades our farmers worked in the marshes, but they have given this up because it means such hard labour, all done by hand. There are not many young people left in Waniewo and the old already have so much to do. Even close to the village there are fields which are not used any more. The farmers have enough land, they don't seek to enlarge their farms and besides, farming nowadays is not very profitable, so for the Waniewo farmers there is no need or wish to drain the marshes."

"I truly hope that the nature of this marsh will be preserved for the future."

large eyes catching the bright light. She suddenly shakes herself, fluffs out and closes one eye. For an instant, time stands still - for an instant only. Far off a cuckoo calls.

Peals of laughter break the peace - some farmers are having a boisterous afternoon break, their fettered ploughhorse grazes on the narrow strip of green between marsh and fields. A magpie drops from a tree and looking for beetles flips over horse-turds. Jackdaws hunt insects on foot around the singly staked and very vociferous cows. The birds take off as a villager passes by, he smiles in greeting but his eyes are wary as he tries to assess my reaction to the pile of fine mesh nets he is carrying. He drops his load into a bright green punt, pushes the boat out and disappears among the towering reeds. He has probably been doing this all his life.

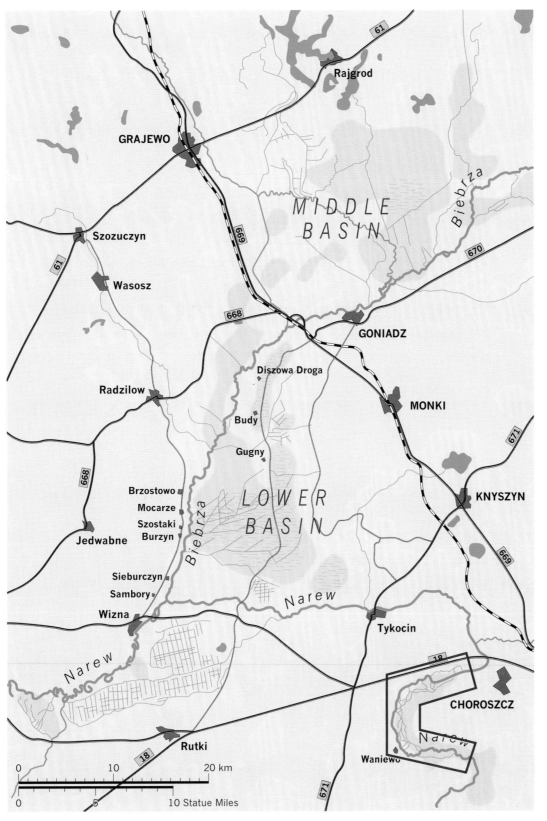

Narew Marsh

A notable feature of the Narew marsh is that many bird species occur which are much rarer in other, comparable marsh habitats. Bittern, little bittern, marsh harrier, water rail, spotted and little crakes, and songbirds as savi's warbler and bluethroat occur in large numbers. Of the 183 species recorded 143 breed here.

Both river and marsh play an important role in the spring migration of waders (black-tailed godwit, ruff, wood sandpiper), and ducks (wigeon, shoveler, garganey and mallard) and lapwing and black-head gull.

The elk is a newcomer, appearing in the late 70's. Other mammals that occur are roe deer, wild boar, badger, fox, otter, beaver, stone marten, hare and musk-rat.

Seventeen species of fish have been recorded, among them roach, pike, ide, tench and burbot.

A large part of the Narew swamp valley still shows natural features, especially between Suraz and Rzedziany, but large tracts have been affected by extensive draining which took place in the early 1980's. According to the North-Podlasie Society for Bird Protection (PTOP) a dozen smaller drainage projects are still being conducted. Drainage has resulted in the loss of more than 50 kilometres of habitat. Big changes have taken place between the villages of Rzedziany and Zóltki (just south of the Warsaw - Bialystok road). Here the water table has been lowered drastically. The level of the river dropped, resulting in a shortening of spring floods: in 1979-81 the floods lasted until May, in 1990 until March and in 1991 only until April.

This has had a marked effect on the numbers of all breeding birds dependent on wet habitat: bitterns have declined from about forty pairs to about ten pairs; black terns have dropped from a thousand to a hundred pairs; savi's warbler from two thousand down to less than four hundred. Bird surveys carried out by PTOP since 1990 have pointed out that less than ten percent of former numbers are to be found.

In an attempt to stop these alarming developments the PTOP has started to buy areas of special interest from farmers. Thanks to financial help from the German-based Society of European Nature Heritage and other foreign conservation organisations and even gifts of land from some farmers, the Society now owns nearly 500 hectares of Narew marshland.

87) *Robert Bateman: 'Narew marsh near Waniewo' - acrylic on board*
   30 x 56.5 cms.

Robert Bateman 1992©

Otter at dawn — Naren River
Poland   May 92
Bruce Pearson

88

89

88) *Bruce Pearson: 'Otter in morning mist' - watercolour 35 x 45 cms.*
89) *Charles Donker: 'Narew marsh' - watercolour 27.5 x 36.5 cms.*

90-91) *Charles Donker: 'Sketchbook pages' - pencil each 26 x 20 cms.*
- "I try to omit more and more as I progress - one can never draw it all. I must develop a way of drawing that comes close to what I see. I am attracted to the landscape when it is overcast, dark and moody."

90

91

"There is hardly a region in Europe that has suffered so much during the past ages as what is now Poland. It has always been a clashing point between east and west, north and south. This has brought forth a history of great sorrow and misery. A land laid waste by the Teutonic Knights, the Swedes, the Tartars, later Napoleon and his armies, the plague, and in the Second World War by the Germans.

There was so much to be seen in Poland, I hardly knew where to begin - I never had to walk far: everywhere I looked there was enough to keep me busy for at least a year.

Finding it difficult to finish my sketches at home I feel compelled to return to the spot where I began again and again. I like to work out of doors, I *need* to work out of doors, I need to feel the atmosphere to get into a certain mood, it is almost like being in a kind of trance.

I have tried to show an unblemished landscape because it contrasts to our western way of life which has taken a direction at the expense of our natural surroundings. Who knows, maybe some kind of technology will be developed to change the direction we've taken - but I seriously doubt it will ever happen…

- *Charles Donker (the Netherlands)*

PENDULINE TITS

For many visitors the ornithological highlight of the boat trips is the penduline tits' nest.

Robert Greenhalf: "A wonderful domed structure apparently made of reedmace 'fluff', presumably bound by cobwebs and suspended from a single wound thread to a branch of a cherry tree, free to swing in the wind. The tits, adding the finishing touches to the nest, were very dapper with pale blue crowns and necks, black face masks and chestnut napes. The rest of their plumage matched the nest colour perfectly."

Bruce Pearson: "At a channel junction I stop for a while watching and sketching as the incomplete pouch of reedmace down is added to. The male arrives suddenly and silently and immediately begins to fidget and fuss inside the swaying pouch, his masked face showing through the holes. Then just as quickly he is away again! For the ten minutes I wait there is no sign of the female."

92) *Vadim Gorbatov: 'Old punt and crayfish traps' - watercolour 30 x 42 cms.*
93) *Robert Greenhalf: 'Punts' - watercolour 35 x 33 cms.*
- "Beautifully shaped and painted, particularly nice when the paint is wearing off revealing previous colours beneath. Flat-bottomed with shallow draught and pointed at both ends, they are ideally designed to push through reed beds."

93

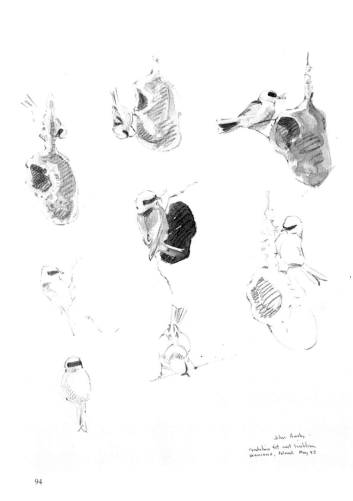

94

95

94) John Busby: 'Penduline tits, sketchbook page' - pencil and watercolour
    31 x 25 cms.
95) Darren Rees: 'Penduline tits' nest' - watercolour 28 x 23 cms.
96) Kim Atkinson: 'Penduline tits at the nest' - watercolour 47 x 24 cms.

Penduline Tit nest,
Waniewo.
96

PHOTO: YSBRAND BROUWERS

"Two weeks was too short a time for me to do anything other than rush about recording places, events and landscape, feeling that I couldn't hope to get all the information I needed. I was most drawn to the meadows beyond the village, the marshes, and the little wood. Because we were living in Waniewo it was important for me to get to know that area as well as possible. In retrospect I wish I had been braver about exploring people's farmyards.

I was sort of pouring it out, just hoping for something good to happen - I'm not quite sure what I was doing, except trying to make sense of impressions and feelings. I still feel I was perched on the surface, seeing it through plate glass. I don't think my work shows any of the problems the area faces; it really just shows how I responded to it as it is *now*.

I like to use the printmaking process, to make results a little more unexpected and exciting. Paintings and prints always seem to start out easy and flowing, then they damp down and I have to get in a state of almost recklessness to be able to do any good at all and get in command again, and achieve the initial simplicity and strength."
- *Kim Atkinson (Wales)*

97

97) *Kim Atkinson: 'Narew marsh' - charcoal and watercolour 30 x 84 cms.*
98) *Robin D'Arcy Shillcock: 'Harriers over Narew marsh' - oil 28 x 40 cms.*

Denis CLAVREUL Sept 1992

100

101

99) *Denis Clavreul: 'Hayricks on Narew marsh' - watercolour 40 x 40 cms.*

100) *John Busby: 'Studies of hayrick, marsh harrier and yellow wagtail' - pencil and watercolour 29 x 20 cms.*
   - Hay is piled around a central pole on a layer of branches so that it stays dry during floods.

101) *Ad Cameron: 'Yellow wagtail' - ink and watercolour 22 x 18 cms.*
   - "I love wide, open landscapes; you can look all around and you even have time to pack your things when it threatens to rain…"

Hans J. Greuse / 1993

102

103

88

102) *Hans Geuze: 'Bittern' - watercolour 46 x 28 cms.*
    - Scattered pairs of bittern begin their breeding activities in the large
    reed beds in the Biebrza and Narew marshes early in spring, sur-
    roundings in which they are extremely hard to spot. The haunting
    night-time call, uttered by the male throughout spring until early
    summer, closely resembles the sound of air being blown across the
    top of an empty bottle; is one of the memorable sounds of the
    marsh. The bird produces the sound by belching inhaled air from its
    stomach into the gizzard.
    In autumn the bitterns from these parts of Poland migrate to areas
    where conditions are less extreme, keeping close to open water
    where they hunt frogs and fish. A sudden drop of temperatures
    accompanied by heavy snowfall may cause many to die of
    exhaustion and starvation.
103) *Chris Rose: 'Hobby above the marsh' - watercolour 29 x 23 cms.*
    - "During the day it became clear that the marsh was not just a place
    of beauty but that it was a place of work for the villagers. Where the
    vilage ended and the marsh began there was no dividing line, no
    fences, one blended into the other."
104) *Jon Fjeldså: 'Snipe among sedge' - watercolour 47.5 x 36 cms.*
    - "I did not intend to show the problems the marsh areas have to
    face, but a small environmental story could be attached to some of
    my work. This painting shows sedge sprouting after winter bur-
    ning. The blue film on the water is caused by iron bacteria, showing
    the presence of ochre in the ground. Changes of land use in the
    future could lead to large-scale ochre pollution downstream."

104

105

105) *Vadim Gorbatov: 'Mallard' - watercolour 43 x 30.5 cms.*
106) *Piet Eggen: 'Study of reeds' - watercolour 25 x 36 cms.*
   - "This small watercolour shows three reed species - actually only
     two, because one shows both the dead, dried form and the new
     shoots of reed-mace."
107) *Victoria Crowe: 'Study of aquatic life' - watercolour 35 x 45 cms.*
   - Around the rhizome and leaves of dragonroot are invertebrates
     such as the marsh snail, believed to pollinate dragonroot.

109

16/5/92

16/5/92

110

108) *Piet Eggen: 'Studies of aquatic life' - pencil and watercolour 38 x 50 cms.*
    - From left to right: water snails, two rudd, a small tench, the head
    of a pike, crayfish, bleak and burbot which lives off crayfish and
    small fish. The dragonfly is a waterdamsel and the plants are water
    violet (left) and water mint (right).
109) *Denis Clavreul: 'Burbot' - pencil and watercolour 16 x 41 cms.*
110) *Robin D'Arcy Shillcock: 'Tench' (detail) - pencil and watercolour*
    30 x 42 cms.

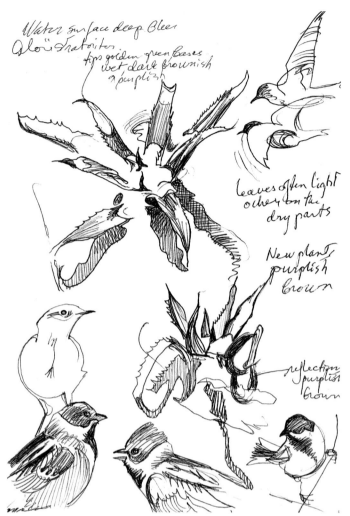

111) Chris Rose: 'Black tern' - watercolour 21 x 29 cms.

112) Jon Fjeldså: 'Sketchbook page with watersoldier, terns and reed bunting' - ballpoint 20.5 x 29 cms.

113) Victoria Crowe: 'Watersoldier' - watercolour 35 x 45 cms.

BLACK TERNS

Winter leaves the marsh almost devoid of life. The marsh is a large, lifeless mat of dead vegetation, of flattened sedge tussocks, reeds bent and broken off below the water line, catching light filtered through water or ice. Harsh winters reach far ahead, affecting the growth of waterplants such as watersoldier, which begin to grow later and are less well developed when black terns look for suitable nesting places early in May.

Black terns favour the watersoldier habitat, which is very rich in insect and invertebrate life, and breed on flimsy mounds of dead plant material that float between its serrated leaves . They hunt above water for small fish and above pastures for insects, but they have also been observed to catch earthworms during very wet spring months.

Since the 19th century the populations of black terns have decreased all over Europe as a result of drainage, land development and water management. But they are also affected by bad conditions in wintering and migration areas and by the indiscriminate use of pesticides in these areas.

Stratiotes-aloides

Victoria Crowe

115

114) *Jon Fjeldså: 'Black terns with watersoldier' - watercolour 23 x 30 cms.*
-"Marsh terns depend on two factors: clear water with submergent plants supporting large diversity of water insects, and on open zones of shoreline which is a favourite feeding area for terns. Grazing keeps the shoreline open, when grazing activity stops it will turn into reed marsh.
Excessive use of fertilizers causes eutrophication and growth of algae, turning the water green. Insect life then becomes dominated by midges and very little other food is available."

115) *Keith Brockie: 'Black tern' - watercolour 37 x 57 cms.*
- Brockie uses a very light sensitive telescope to make detailed portraits, with an emphasis on small details that characterize the individual animal. "For any painter of wild birds and animals the most important piece of equipment is an extension of one's eyes - preferably a telescope."[9]

117

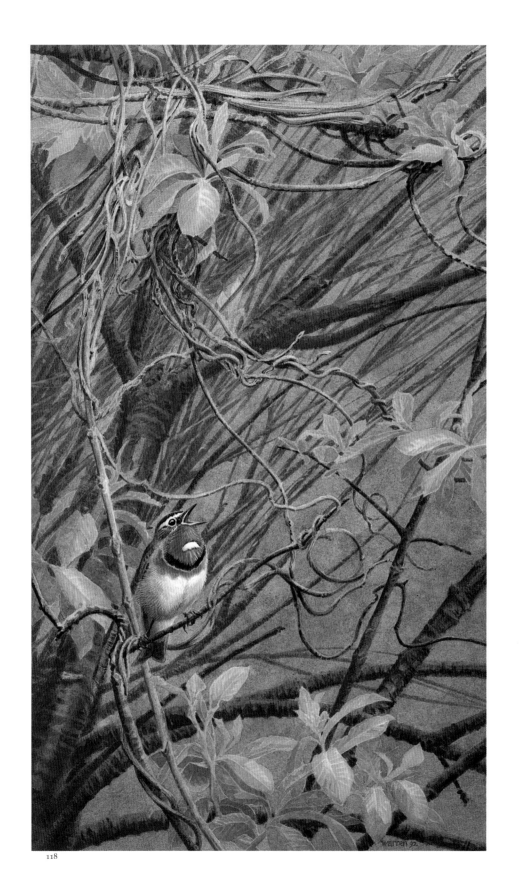

118

116) *Jean Chevallier: 'Black terns' - charcoal and watercolour 36.5 x 51 cms.*
- "During a trip like this I tend to profit as much as possible from being in the field by accumulating quick, uncomposed sketches and watercolours based on field observations."
117) *Dag Peterson: 'Jackdaw' - lithograph 31 x 25 cms.*
118) *Michael Warren: 'Bluethroat' - watercolour 40 x 23.5 cms.*

Rosefinches
LB McQueen
May 1992

119

119) *Lawrence McQueen: 'Scarlet rosefinches' - watercolour 21 x 27 cms.*
   - "On the last day of my stay I watched a male display to a female working on the seeds, taking full advantage of the sunlight to reflect his bright colours."

120) *Mike Warren: 'Great snipe, Waniewo' - watercolour 29 x 12.5 cms.*
   - "Although we visited the great snipe lek in the Biebrza area we also witnessed the ritual at a smaller lek on the edge of Waniewo. I spent several evenings with these birds; the 15th was a moonlit night and I sketched the birds and absorbed the atmosphere. I painted the scene next day - it was strange sheltering from the sun beneath a tree, and painting a night scene."

120

121) *Keith Brockie: 'Long-eared owl' - pencil 30 x 25 cms.*
122) *Andrew Haslen: 'Ortolan bunting' - pencil and watercolour 30 x 41 cms.*
123) *Vadim Gorbatov: 'Narew by moonlight - beaver' - watercolour
     38 x 51 cms.*

- "The moon rises above the horizon and bathes the reeds and quiet channels in a cool light. I've been waiting near a beaver lodge for a long time, hoping to see a beaver. I've found a dry seat on an old burl among waterways and bushes. The warm May night is full of calling thrush nightingales, croaking frogs and from somewhere a bittern can be heard. A swish of wings and a late mallard hits the water, shattering the moon's reflection. Quacking softly the drake leaves the scene, but the moon's reflection is now slightly marred by the buzzing flight of insects. I wonder if the lodge has been abandoned but if so, why are there white shavings lying around?
There - a soft splash, a beaver cleaves the surface - and another one! They disappear momentarily, then surface together, leaving a trail of bubbles, all in absolute silence… A sudden whack! of a tail makes me jerk in fright. I lose balance and fall into the channel! Regaining my previous position with waterlogged boots and dripping clothes, I immediately start shivering and decide to leave, having to make my way through the vegetation to the distant firelight of our camp - where there is laughter and singing. Someone pulls up a log and I remove my boots, stretch my feet to the warmth of the blaze while someone else pours me a glass of vodka."

123

THE BIEBRZA VALLEY

"He who lives among silence becomes the centre of a world."
- Theodore Rousseau[10]

The photographer's aerial pictures show a plain composed of interlocking shapes divided by the Biebrza River: a ribbon, at times dark and ominous or sparkling like a thread of burnished silver laid out in a weird succession of twists and bends, in places doubling back on itself to form a perfect noose around small islands of shrubs. Elongated pools and kidney-shaped ponds, scattered around the main stream like pieces of a puzzle, are evidence of a laborious course no longer followed.

A closer scrutiny reveals much detail: settlements with u-shaped farmyards surrounded by trees and connected to each other by long roads; paths radiating from farms to irregular patches of cultivated land; the subtle shading of vegetation: reed beds, sedge moor, a dense cover of water lilies on backwaters; sallow bordering along waterways and long, yellow strips of marsh-marigolds. One picture shows a group of storks put to flight by the photographer's plane; I count thirty birds in a spark-like pattern above water that reflects the sun's midday glare.

The photographer captures it all in one image: the river, the land, its inhabitants - each aerial view an image of great abstract beauty.

Standing on the spur of the moraine overlooking what the Frenchman Jean Chevallier called "a dream of paradise" we joke with each other, point out distant birds and stuff our hands deep in coat pockets. The first day out with the group of artists proves to be a cold, wet day full of anticipation, expectation. We have escaped from the bus and its steamed up windows which severely restricted our view of paradise, to get this first panoramic view of the Biebrza.

A group of male ruffs comes over, low and fast like fighter planes, we crouch over our telescopes but they disappear from sight somewhere over the river's floodplain.

At this point it shimmers through tall stands of trees. Originating more than a hundred kilometres to the northeast, close to the border with White Russia, the river appears from haze and disappears from view into a white haze in the south; its disappearance final when Biebrza waters join with the Narew, twisting, turning, tumbling, until what is Biebrza and what is Narew cannot be divided.

Between source and confluence the river passes through time, its passage marking, as it were, periods of history: flowing from its source it passes through a 20th century landscape, through marshland drained and cultivated, the wilderness subjugated. In the middle reaches it passes land marked by 19th century drainage canals, the wilderness threatened but still dominant. In the south, between the town of Goniadze and our vantage point - near Sambory - the landscape lies unchanged since medieval times, undisturbed since the beginning of history.

During the last ice age massive glaciers scoured the landscape, pushing up the ridge on which we now stand; as the glaciers retreated accumulations of debris were left on the valley floor, elevations which escaped the influence of floodwater, islands on which woods could develop. These old woods are the favoured nesting sites for white-tailed and lesser spotted eagles, the wary black stork and the eagle owl.

The mires have always been an impenetrable wilderness for man, the floods as much a deterrent as his ingrained fear of the evil he believed lurked in the marsh. Even today man shies away from the trouble involved in trekking into the deeper reaches of the Biebrza marshes, not out of fear but simply because he has no pressing reason to visit the inaccessible places - where one of the rarest of European mammals, the wolf, still has its territory.

125

124) *Biebrza near Sosnia. Photo: Wiktor Wolkow.* 125) *Biebrza near Joje - Awissa. Photo: Wiktor Wolkow.*

126

Animals rely on the isolation from human interference offered by marshes and by the floods which hold the land in their grip for months. For ages the river has had its own way of coping with the onslaught of water: its meanders slowing down the gush coming down its main course and the bogs acting as a sponge, absorbing excess water. In the southern part of the Biebrza called the Lower Basin, the overflow dynamics are extensive because man-made drainage systems are absent, so that low-nutritive, calcium-rich seepage water can flow into the valley from the foot of the sand ridge that offers such a beautiful view of the valley.

The resulting floods determine where migrating birds will find security to rest and feed and also affect the numbers of breeding birds from year to year: an area rich in spotted crake or white-winged black terns one year may be devoid of these birds the next if the waterlevel is too high, or too low.

The Biebrza landscape is an environment formed and dominated by the constant movement of water, forcing plants to adapt to changing conditions and producing shifting patterns of their distribution. In the areas flooded annually by the river only reeds and tall sedge communities dominate, while in the areas outside the inundation zone the dominating plant groups are moss and short sedge communities. The dividing line between these two zones cannot be sharply drawn. Instead they are bound by a wide belt of different habitats which are only sporadically affected by floods, but kept wet by seepage water. Here plant communities can be found in various stages of development and degeneration.

The mowing of moist meadows late in summer and grazing cows, horses and geese have helped create areas which are interesting for birds such as ruff, godwit and snipe. In the Biebrza Valley spring migrants have come to rely on the meadows surrounded by water where the vegetation is still short from the previous year's haymaking.

Bruce Pearson: "In Burzyn a cobbled track leads from the village square around a farm busy in mid-morning milking. Skirting an orchard heavy with blossom the track leads down to the marsh. The view is open with wet meadows, rush shallows and sedge fens running out towards islands of sallow and sheets of open water close to where the main river runs."

"There is almost too much to draw so I settle to paint a landscape to calm me down. The day is bright and warm with a steady breeze, and there is a feast of birdlife here. Dozens of black and white-winged black terns are feeding where recent floodwater has covered a meadow. Further out a cluster of ruff are feeding, fabulously adorned in full breeding plumage - and there's a wood sandpiper too. Every line of broken fence posts has a singing yellow wagtail, some posts are topped by watching redshanks or

black-tailed godwits. Marsh harriers drift by, and then high overhead, a lesser spotted eagle."

"By lunchtime I have notes on whiskered tern, black stork, crane, Montague's harrier, sea eagle and hobby, among others in my notebook. But best of all is a flurry of red-footed falcons, obviously on passage - three or four of them at once, high up and spread out on the wind which carries them up the valley, feeding on the wind as they go."

Three of us make our way through swampy alder forest, jumping across narrow channels of stagnant, black water and using tree trunks for support and protruding hummocks as stepping stones. We are embarrassed by our own noise; we separate upon reaching open terrain.

I spend a day in a wooden tower, looking at rectangular portions of the surrounding terrain. Rain drifting in causes my paper to buckle and a brush falls between the floor boards. Snipe drum in a part of the sky I cannnot see and I hear the territory call of corncrakes all through the day, its sound closely resembling a comb moved across an empty matchbox. *Crex crex* - a beautiful scientific name, resembling its call, short and surprising as the bird itself. They are impossible to see, impossible to pinpoint: when calling corncrakes turn their heads the call sounds alternatively distant and near. "…the strange almost crude cry of corncrakes, a sudden mysterious croak from across the marsh followed by the queerest of silences," H.E. Bates wrote in *Down the River*.[11]

An elk appears and browses among the already stunted birches, the protruding knobs on its head marking it as a young bull. It moves back into cover after a while, but reappears to continue feeding. I want to draw Vadim's attention, but he is invisible in his tower a few hundred metres away.

Vadim Gorbatov: "I'm laying on the boards of a highseat, feeling fine.The wind keeps the mosquitoes away and dries my soggy boots. Above me spotted eagles circle in the sky, now and again they grapple with each other, it's part of their bridal flight."

"Hearing a splashing sound beneath me I see elk which have come very near, their strange bearded heads and rounded muzzles clearly visible, and the long ears, the stringy hair on their shoulders and the dark red hair of their wintercoats which they are beginning to lose. They are clumsy, lumbering animals, but show strength and grace in their flowing long strides! As ghosts they disappear and the silence returns, a silence filled with bird song."

Another day spent in a different tower in another part of the eastern Biebrza Valley. I have now chosen the highseat as a refuge from all the people moving around the fenland of Kozli Rynek, famous for its daylight lek of great snipe. Foreign bird watchers with telescopes dot the

127

126) *The Biebrza lower basin.* 127) *Reedbeds, lower basin.*

128-129) *Lower basin.*

track and German university students work among the
sedge depositing samples of the peat bottom in plastic
canisters, labelled and dated for laboratory research on
the food of fenland birds. The tall figure of Bruce Pearson,
who almost shook me from my seat when he clambered
up my tower a little while ago, is on his way to another
tower partly hidden by sallow. He makes good time
across the moorland and as he merges into the yellow
green trees the dark silhouette of an elk moves away in
the opposite direction.

Looking through slits at the sunlit landscape. Two golden orioles shoot across the rectangle I'm peering through
- the brightest yellow I have ever seen in any bird. Later a
black stork glides into view. There is something about this
wary stork which makes it appear more 'chic' than the
white stork, the all-black plumage relieved by white when
it opens its beautifully pinioned wings, the red on leg,
beak and around eye made all the more striking by the
black. It looks - oriental.

Vadim Gorbatov: "At dusk an enormous red moon
looms over the marsh. Short-eared owls glide silently by.
Our landrover bumps and lurches through the holes, the
headlights picking out tightly packed spruce trees in the
dark - a pair of bright red eyes glow in the dark. While we
try to guess what it could be, a nightjar rises from the
track and disappears into darkness."

Czerwone Bagno, the Red Marsh in the Middle Basin,
is reached by a road that runs between drained fields and
pastures on one hand and wet forest on the other. This is
an area for lesser spotted eagles, cranes, black stork,
white-backed woodpeckers and even hoopoe. From the
forest an old female goshawk, lying low on her nest, gla-
res at us with wild, orange eyes. The villages are strung
out along the roadside: Stoczek, Ciszewo and finally
Kuligi; from here we walk the last few kilometres through
dry woodland and abandoned meadows on a glacial
deposit until we arrive at a ridge giving a view towards
the southwest. There the group disperses.

Two cranes, pure silver in the white light, drop from the sky and as they bank I can see a ripple of coverts on their broad wings. They land behind birches spreading out from the ridge and stalk gracefully across the moor.

I plod across the sodden marsh, struggling to keep an even pace on the lumpy tussocks. It is slow going and I'm pleased to come upon a narrow trail made by elk, so I splash down its course even though it takes me away from my intended direction and into the cover of low birches. Finding a spot no different from any other, but with a distinct different feel, I spread my gear on the dry sedge and begin to draw -*try* to draw- the pure white of the birches. Cranes trumpet nearby, the sound clear despite the rustle of the birches. Somehow their sound is reassuring, giving me the feeling I have all the time in the world.

A sound, lighter than the wind. I have been dreaming and squint at the radiance on everything touched by the afternoon light. Slightly to the side of me, a wheatear perches on taut legs, dark toes gripping the dried stem of wood angelica. We are both surprised. We wait. My eyes move up to touch the softness of the feathering on its breast, the pulsating throat, and from above a ball of fluff that hides the beak one dark eye holds my gaze.

These small encounters are imbued with a force of life I cannot forget. In Czerwone Bagno the light, and the fact that I am alone among a million stalks of sedge, has its effect. As does the presence of water underneath a sea of sedge that crackles in dryness. Bending low to study the progress of a beetle I can smell the water as it slowly oozes up to my ankles from the peaty soil.

Towards the end of the afternoon I regain the sand dune in a kind of trance, eyes feeling loose in their sockets. "What did you see?" they ask. I have no answer. The air is very still, low trees stretch into the distance, hiding the river from view.

Lawrence McQueen: "I was deeply moved by the beauty of the Biebrza Valley. Watching the daily rhythm of human lives around the villages and fields against the background of river and marsh, I sensed a kind of balance in this landscape, a symmetry that embraces both the cultivated and the natural landscape of wetland and forest. The two are separate environments, yet one is richer for the other. When I looked at the soil, worked by horse and plow to the very threshold of village houses, and saw that human figures on this land are shaped by their efforts to transform this soil into sustenance, it became apparent to me that the soil, created by this river and these marshes, is central to this symmetry.

This is a landscape of serene beauty, for it is harmoniously life-endowed. Yet this remnant of earlier times becomes illusory under the threat of modern development."

130

131

130) *Lower basin, from sandy ridge.* 131) *Stork.*

132

132) *Bog forest, near the Czar's road (lower basin).*

THE BIEBRZA VALLEY

Snaking from its source near the Polish-Russian border, the river covers 160 kilometres of valley before joining the Narew near the village of Sambory. River and floodplain may reach a width of two kilometres of waterways and stagnant pools in a valley two to fifteen kilometres wide, totalling 90,000 ha.

The flora is very diverse even though the vegetation period is short between winter and flooding in spring. Forty-five plant communities have been identified in a variety of habitats; besides low flora communities such as sedge, moss-sedge and moist meadow communities also boreal and even glacial flora can be found.

The valley can be subdivided into three areas, diversity of habitat and species increasing towards the south: the first 35 kilometres of the river lie in the **upper or northern basin,** an area of 9000 ha without any conservation status. Here the marsh has been drained and turned into pasture-land and hay-meadows, what is left of fen- and moss marshes is annually burned by landowners trying to get rid of scrubgrowth.

The **middle basin** (40,000 ha) consists of a broad peat area, about 33 kilometres long and up to 24 kilometres wide, with dunes and sand drifts covered with vegetation. Early in the 19th century parts of the marsh were drained and meanders of tributaries cut short by the Augustowski, Woznawiejski and Rudzki canals, built for strategic and economic reasons. Water taken over a much shorter stretch of land causes erosion and a drop of the level of groundwater, causing a change of habitat in adjacent areas: the peat bogs dry out and are covered by willow and birch scrub. In winters without snow fires may break out destroying surface vegetation. Bushfires in summers with a low waterlevel are more serious because peat layers are ignited and difficult to extinguish when smouldering. In 1992 bushfires devastated over 3000 hectares in the middle and lower basins, destroying rodent and invertebrate populations.

Of the middle basin an area of 11,200 ha has been designated a peat reserve called Czerwone Bagno or Red Marsh, situated between the Augustowski and Woznawiejski canals.

Lower or southern basin: 35 kilometres of river and 30,000 ha of valley characterized by broad inundation zones. In the lower basin man has had little influence on the marshes and peat bogs which are dominated by river overflow and seepage water from the high terrain around the valley. The unaltered ground water level gives the vegetation a chance to regenerate naturally.

Of the 235 species of birds recorded 157 are breeding birds and another 19 are possible breeders. The Biebrza is a stronghold for many Central European species e.g. eagle owl (about 24 pairs), short-toed eagle (2 pairs), crane (200 pairs), water rail (up to 1500 pairs), spotted crake (between 800 and 1600 pairs), corncrake (up to 2000 pairs), and white-winged black tern, aquatic warbler and wigeon.

Thirty-five species of fresh water fish have been identified. Among them bream, ide, chub, wels, minnow, crucian carp, stone loach, gudgeon and lampern.

Beyond the fenland lie large tracts of wet birch and alder forest, and on higher terrain pine and spruce forests in which the larger mammals find adequate cover and rest during winter. Various mammals occur such as elk (or moose), red deer, roe deer, wild boar, badger, beaver, otter, wolf and raccoon dog, which has spread from the east over the past decade. Rodents include water and pygmy shrews, northern birch mouse, hazel dormouse and root vole.

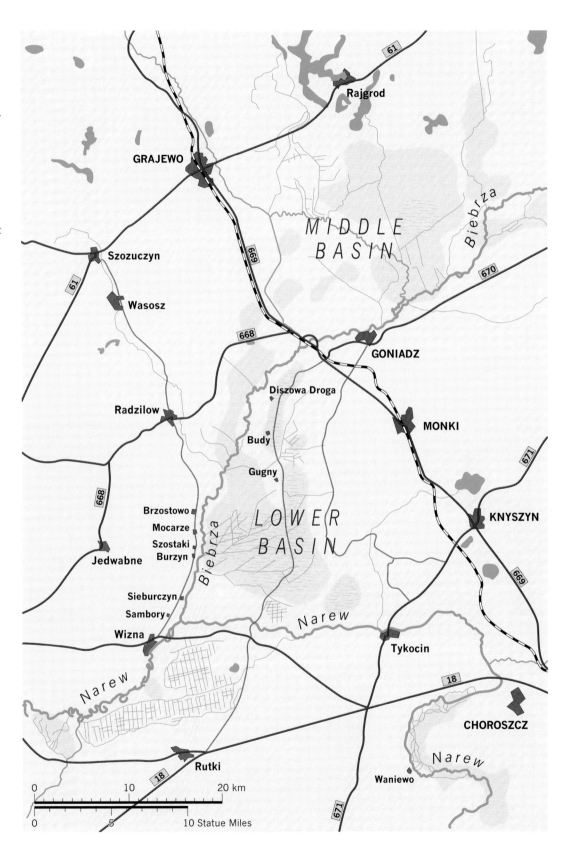

133

135

133) *Peter Partington: 'The Biebrza Valley' - watercolour 46 x 113 cms.*

134) *John Busby: 'Birds of the Biebrza' - pencil and watercolour 30 x 40 cms.*
    - "Most lasting images - the aerial slides of the marshes made by
    Wiktor Wolkow, the marsh itself at dawn and dusk and lots of
    miniature images of birds - the thrill of new species like black stork
    and lesser spotted eagle, aquatic warbler and scarlet rosefinch. The
    freedom from car and plane noise, the freshness of the air."
    Species shown are stork, terns, a pochard, ruff and swallow.

135) *Siegfried Woldhek: 'The Biebrza, from Sieburczyn' - watercolour*
    21 x 29 cms.
    - "Along this river that winds, separates and comes together,
    marshes, peatbogs, woods can be found. Here one finds everything
    that once existed in most of Europe. While painting the light keeps
    changing so much and because of that colours and forms change, so
    that one has to address one's senses and analytical powers in a
    special way. Compared to that drawing portraits is easy."

137

136) *Bruce Pearson: 'Biebrza landscape' - mixed media 40.5 x 57 cms.*
137) *Denis Clavreul: 'Haystacks' - pencil and watercolour 30 x 41 cms.*

138) *Michael Warren: 'Ruffs near Zoslowo' - watercolour 27 x 22 cms.*
- "A very hot day. Many ruffs still moving through this part of the marsh. A small group stayed most of the day and occasionally indulged in lekking activity. Some birds appeared tired and rested on the fringe of the group. The lekking birds presented a wonderful visual spectacle…"

139) *Vadim Gorbatov: 'At the edge of the Biebrza' - watercolour 31 x 43 cms.*
- The tracks of the horse-drawn carts made in winter can be seen, and on a fence-post a yellow wagtail, mute swans and in the distance a barge for transporting cattle. On the bow of the punt in the foreground lie the punctured remains of frogs left by an otter.

140) *Bruce Pearson: 'The Biebrza' - mixed media 40 x 50 cms.*

140

THE BIEBRZA VALLEY

142

141

141) *Jon Fjeldså: 'Ruffs' - watercolour 23 x 31 cms.*
    - Ruffs return each year to the same sites along the Biebrza to enact their communal display rituals. Many of the birds are on their way to the northern tundra, but some breed locally on sedge marsh and on moist hay meadows. Three males are shown, two with distended head adornments.The birds have small territories and start to 'fight' when one bird invades the territory of another. In the background there is a female or 'reeve'.

142) *Andrew Haslen: 'Dandelions and ruff' - pencil and watercolour 57 x 78 cms.*

143) *Chris Rose: 'Cranes, lower basin' - oil on panel.*
    - "The painting produced after returning home was inspired by a scene late one afternoon: I settled down to a painting of a moored punt. As time wore on I became aware of the sound of distant cranes, gathered on the far side of the water. Some fifty birds were busy feeding and displaying, the afternoon sun came out and the stage was set! These graceful birds appeared to me like dancers, or actors, and I wanted to convey an impression of players on a stage. I managed to fill two or three pages with sketches before the waiting bus called me away."

143

144

144) *Michael Warren: 'Thrush nightingale' - watercolour 30 x 18 cms.*
145) *Jon Fjeldså: 'Black-tailed godwits' - watercolour 30.5 x 18 cms.*
146) *Chris Rose: 'Punt on the Biebrza' - watercolour 29 x 21 cms.*

145

Chris Rose

146

148

147) *Victoria Crowe: 'Riverine water crowfoot' - watercolour 24 x 31.5 cms.*
   - From her sketchbook: "…an enjoyment of the structure and beauty
   of some of of the water plants - just wonderfully complex things to
   draw. I see them as a separate activity which is a kind of widening
   of my knowledge. I try to choose things representative of the
   marshes."
148) *Denis Clavreul: 'Water avens' - pencil and watercolour 30 x 41 cms.*
149) *Jean Chevallier: 'Marsh trefoil or bogbean' - charcoal and watercolour
   32 x 24 cms.*

149

151

150) *Alan Johnston: 'Plants of the southern basin' - pencil and watercolour*
46 x 31 cms.
- Top: left to right: marsh violet, alternate-leaved saxifrage, water avens. Below: common horsetail, yellow deadnettle, field woodrush and greater pond sedge.

151) *Victoria Crowe: 'Plants of the sandy ridge near Sambory' - watercolour*
35 x 45 cms.
- Top: left to right: wild strawberry and forget-me-nots, bitter milkwort and field bugloss. Below: stork's bill, field pansy, hairy speedwell and white mouse-eared chickweed.
- "The flower studies are an attempt to sort through the species and also to see the whole event as a series of enjoyable personal discoveries, with enough clues to the identity of the flowers as seen en masse, without making botanical illustrations."

152

153

152) *Hans Geuze: 'Swans' - watercolour 36 x 52 cms.*
   - "Returning to Holland I once again noticed how poor nature is in
   the rich countries in the west and how cosmetic the measures taken
   by governments blinded by economic progress. The enormous
   contrast between the small-scale agriclulture in Poland and dying
   nature here in Holland will always remain with me."
153) *Tomasz Cofta: 'Female reed bunting' - gouache 18 x 13 cms.*
154) *Michael Warren: 'White-winged and black terns, near Burzyn' -*
   watercolour 30 x 23 cms.
   - "A flock of terns, predominantly white-winged blacks, were
   feeding over wet areas of marsh. The birds were superb in their
   black and white plumage above the glittering water. They moved in
   a ceaseless flow, coming in, dipping to feed, lifting away and
   returning to the rear of the flock. It was a sunny but windy day. In
   the afternoon rain stopped painting and I had to return next day to
   complete the picture."

154

White-winged black terns

"A storm of black and white-winged black terns dipping over the water…" is how Keith Brockie described our first close view of a group of both species searching for food above wind-swept water near the town of Goniadze. Quite a few artists returned to the site to study the birds better. Robert Greenhalf: "A rather surreal experience was painting terns to the accompaniment of Madonna blaring from a nearby campsite at Goniadze. This was more disturbing to me and Chris Rose than to the birds."

Though often seen together when feeding both species breed in separate colonies in the Biebrza area. The population of white-winged black terns - an exceptionally ugly name for a graceful bird - is probably the most numerous in Central Europe, varying between 140 and 475 breeding pairs. The white-winged blacks build their nests in sedge marsh which is inundated, but well away from the river itself.

155) *Robert Greenhalf: 'White-winged black terns' - watercolour 25 x 33 cms.*
- "A fine, windy day spent with Denis Clavreul by the riverside. The birds patrolled the river surface upon which the wind, current and reflected clouds all played to provide endlessly new patterns and configurations."

156) *Jean Chevallier: 'White-winged black terns' - charcoal and watercolour 37 x 52 cms.*

157) *Denis Clavreul: 'White-winged black terns' - pencil heightened with white.*

156

157

158

158) *Denis Clavreul: 'Ermine and spotted crake studies' - pencil and watercolour 30 x 41 cms.*

159) *Bruce Pearson: 'Black stork over fen landscape' - mixed media 42 x 60 cms.*
- Sketches of the sedge moor of the southern basin and Montague's harrier, black stork, and observations on birds and the appearance of the vegetation.

Black Stork

159

GREAT SNIPE

The populations of great snipe in Poland belong to the southernmost fringe of the bird's distribution, which reaches to the far north of Russia. In the Biebrza about 400 displaying males have been counted, the largest number in Central Europe. It is a slightly heavier and fuller-bodied bird than the common snipe, its flight when flushed straighter than the zigzag flight of the smaller bird.

The great snipe is faithful to sites along its migration route and to the communal lek where several birds can display together. It arrives in eastern Poland in late April well after the common snipe. There are several areas in the Biebrza and the Narew area where lekking birds can be observed, some of these display sites have been leased or bought by PTOP.

Bruce Pearson's description of snipe activity at the lek: "…I set up my portable studio and begin the wait. Cranes are feeding at the far edge of the fen and male Montague's harrier quarters the area for a while. Suddenly, deep in the vegetation forty yards ahead of me there's a sharp metallic purring sound that builds for a few seconds, then ends abruptly - the first snipe is on the lek. In a while there are several birds calling, but it is difficult to see how many birds there are and what is going on. The lek is in deep tussock grass, but now and then a running or fluttering bird is visible and sometimes the flash of white in wings and tail shows. As the light fades the intensity of sound on the lek grows and by the time I am groping for my things, the birds are at full tilt."

161

162

160) *Kim Atkinson: 'Great snipe displaying' - watercolour 27 x 111 cms.*

161) *Kim Atkinson: 'Great snipe at the lek' - 77 x 56 cms.*

- "The most special thing was hearing the great snipe at their lek. I feel quite nervous that increased numbers of bird watchers will affect these, and the black terns, godwits and aquatic warblers. Tourism may have an adverse effect on many things we would all like to see preserved - aren't we helping to spread that to the area? It's easy to get despondent when you are away from there and looking at it with a wider point of view. The paintings may have a dreamlike quality because of their exaggerated colours and the fragility of the paper; the tears and patches may say something about the precariousness of it all."

162) *Andrew Haslen: 'Great snipe' - pencil and watercolour 78 x 57 cms.*

163

164

165

"A lasting impression is of the tranquility of the Biebrza. It was travelling back in time to a slower and quieter age, feeling that parts of Britain were like that once and we have lost them.

I researched the birds of Biebrza to establish key species to concentrate on, birds being selected for reasons of rarity, peculiar to the area or having personal appeal. I would not go to Poland to paint birds I see regularly in Nottinghamshire. I am aware that the bird watcher in me dictates subject matter. My paintings show and celebrate various species that would be threatened by damage to existing environment.

There was an abundance of subject matter, but what was occasionally difficult was getting close to a particular bird in such a vast area. Otherwise the meeting exceeded my expectations, probably because I was afflicted by pre-trip apprehension…

The days were long: often from 5.30 am to 11 pm and later. Inevitably I was running out of steam towards the end.

I would like to do more field painting, as a matter of balance with work that ties me to the studio. I spend a lot of time in the field birding, but that is a relaxation from work and does not always involve drawing."

- Michael Warren (England)

163) *Denis Clavreul: 'Displaying great snipe' - conté and chalk 24.5 x 32 cms.*

164) *Jean Chevallier: 'Great snipe' - charcoal and watercolour 30 x 36 cms.*

165) *David Daly: 'Great snipe displaying' - watercolour 27 x 35 cms.*

166-167) *Michael Warren: 'Studies from sketchbook' - coloured pencil
    each 20 x 14 cms.*

AQUATIC WARBLER

An estimated 2500 to 3500 pairs breed in the marshes of the Biebzra, making it the most important breeding area in Europe for this passerine. The total population spread throughout the former Soviet Union, with isolated pockets in Poland and in the Danube delta, is estimated at about 8000 pairs. Loss of wetland due to drainage and waterlevel regulation has caused the aquatic warbler to disappear as a breeder from all of Western Europe, so the Biebrza population can be said to be of international importance.

It is a secretive little warbler, rather heavily marked on back and head, with a light bar like a parting down the middle of its crown - the distinguishing feature when compared to all other Acrocephalus warblers. It favours peat bog overgrown with tussocky sedge, areas that border on the zone that is flooded annually.

169

170

168) *Larry Barth: 'Aquatic warbler' - polyform and acrylic, height with base:*
    45 cms.
169) *Tomasz Cofta: 'Aquatic warbler' - gouache 14 x 16 cms.*
170) *David Daly: 'Studies of aquatic warbler' - watercolour 28 x 37 cms.*

171

172

171) *David Daly: 'Aquatic warbler' - watercolour 35 x 28 cms.*
 - "The aquatic warblers and great snipe were highlights for me - but to do them justice would have taken many more hours of observation."
172) *Michael Warren: 'Aquatic warbler' - watercolour 26 x 26 cms.*
173) *Robin D'Arcy Shillcock: 'Corncrakes all around' - pencil and watercolour 29 x 41.5 cms.*

173

175

174

174) *Jean Chevallier: 'Marsh harrier over the lower basin. Drawn from a hide' - charcoal and watercolour 38 x 52 cms.*

175) *Charles Donker: 'Birches, lower basin' - watercolour 28 x 38 cms.*

176) *Vadim Gorbatov: 'Elk cow and calves' - watercolour 47.5 x 69.5 cms.*
- "At the edge of a wood, between some willow trees and skinny birches an elk cow browses, moving unhurriedly from one spot to another. When she lies down she is completely out of sight. Close by a pair of cranes feed, pause and preen. Both cranes and elk feel safe here, protected by open space and the sogginess of the ground. My eyes are attracted by a movement in the high grass behind the elk cow, long ears and a sandy coloured back become visible - a calf! It joins its mother after having slept, tripping over the vegetation. Hungrily it bumps her in the groin while in the distance, in air wavering in the heat, the cranes are dancing, their cries coming down on the wind to me, a witness of their secret life."

176

177) *Vadim Gorbatov: 'Cranes and elk' - watercolour 43 x 61 cms.*
178) *Vadim Gorbatov: 'Elks' - watercolour 31 x 43 cms.*

177

178

Elk

During the Second World War the elk almost became extinct, but the population recovered in the years after the war, because of the absence of hunting. In 1967 hunting was resumed, reducing the number of elk to about 300. Elk are important in keeping the growth of scrub on the marshes and moors in check. In winter they cause damage to forests by browsing on small trees. In the upper basin where there are very few elks roe deer and red deer help in keeping scrub down.

179

180

179) *Jean Chevallier: 'Elk' - charcoal and watercolour 20 x 27 cms.*
180) *Andrew Haslen: 'Elk' - pencil and watercolour 56 x 78 cms.*
   - "My first moose, so big and prehistoric, standing on the other side of a clearing. More than anything else I wanted to convey this, but my sketches were slight and held little information."
181) *Vadim Gorbatov: 'A full moon above the marsh' - watercolour 33 x 47 cms.*

"I like to work in nature because the surrounding nature seeps into my sketches, if I want it to or not. The more valuable material is that which conveys the living impressions. At first I looked around and drew whatever crossed my path, but I soon turned my attention to elks and cranes, spending all the time available in the areas where they occurred.

Thinking back of the marshes that remind me of the tundra of the Russian north, I have many lasting impressions, especially of the endless space, of large groups of birds wheeling above the marsh, of skies reflected in water. Blues and greens, speckled with the bright yellow of dandelions.

I don't believe an artist can influence the solutions to ecological, or social, problems - as soon as he tries to do that, his work becomes edifying and boring…

But art that is sincere will bring the artist's love for his surroundings across to other people who maybe fail to see the beauty. Only in this way can an artist contribute to the solution of problems of society - but it is a process that takes time and often produces disappointing results."

- Vadim Gorbatov (Russia)

181

182

183

184

182) *Darren Rees: 'Cranes' - watercolour 30.5 x 40 cms.*
 - In Poland the crane has declined as marshland disappeared, but it is a common bird in the Biebrza area which supports a population of nearly 200 pairs, the largest population in Central Europe.

183) *Lawrence McQueen: 'Whinchat' - watercolour 25 x 24 cms.*

184) *Andrew Haslen: 'Whinchat' - pencil and watercolour 32 x 26 cms.*
 - A compact passerine often perched upright on exposed perches. Of its song Charles Donker said "A light warble that fits this landscape of tenuous stems of reeds and sedge perfectly…"

185) *David Daly: 'Studies of shrike and young at nest' - pencil and watercolour 25 x 35 cms.*

185

186

186) *Kim Atkinson: 'Shrike feeding young' - watercolour 55 x 37 cms.*
187) *Kim Atkinson: 'Treecreeper' - watercolour 56 x 37 cms.*
188) *Vadim Gorbatov: 'Woodcock' - watercolour 70 x 47 cms.*

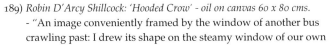

189) *Robin D'Arcy Shillcock: 'Hooded Crow' - oil on canvas 60 x 80 cms.*
   - "An image conveniently framed by the window of another bus crawling past: I drew its shape on the steamy window of our own bus, mentally fixing the image.
   I continued to remove elements from the composition until something remained which reminded me of the spikiness of the dead corvids hanging everywhere and the soft contours of the landscape around the Biebrza Valley."
190) *Keith Brockie: ' Roebuck (Middle Basin)' - pencil 30 x 25 cms.*
191) *Vadim Gorbatov: 'Goshawk takes hooded crow' - watercolour 61 x 43 cms.*

group of orchids
and horse tails
growing in a mossy
clump in the eastern
part of the Spearum
Basin

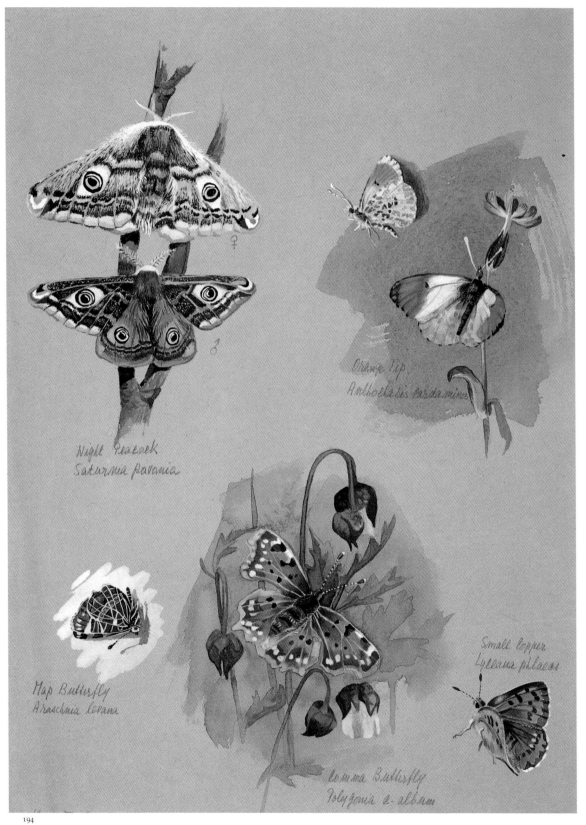

194

195

192) *Victoria Crowe: 'Spotted orchids and horsetails, eastern part of lower basin' - watercolour 45 x 35 cms.*
193) *Piet Eggen: 'Spotted orchid from eastern, part of lower basin' - watercolour 51 x 36 cms.*
194) *Hans Geuze: 'Biebrza butterflies I' - watercolour 45 x 30 cms.*
   - Top: night peacock, orange tip. Bottom: map butterfly, comma butterfly and small copper.
   - "The birds and butterflies I painted say something of the extensively grazed low-nutricient pastures with dozens of forms of higher and lower plantlife. Nostalgia - these habitats have disappeared in Holland."
195) *Hans Geuze: 'Biebrza butterflies II' - watercolour 33 x 25 cms.*
   - Left, top to bottom: orange tip, comma, red admiral and map butterfly. Right, top to bottom: Macroglossum spec, grizzled skipper and camberwell beauty.

196

THROUGH THE EYES OF STRANGERS

"The eye grows more enquiring and exact, the sensibility, though no keener, is more subtly attuned, drawing seems to probe more deeply, the powers of observation increase. Nature, under this close scrutiny, reveals detail on detail, incident and variation without end."
- Eugène Fromentin (1820 -1876) [12]

Sunday. During the informal exhibition we have put up for the villagers in the draughty barn in the centre of Waniewo, a farmer rubs his stubby finger across a carefully delineated roe deer head drawn by Keith Brockie, no doubt telling the Scotsman of his encounters with these dainty animals. Beyond the dark interior of the barn spring seems to sparkle through the cracks in the walls; chickens draw attention as they move from light into shade, and back into light again below rows of drawings suspended from wires stretched along the walls. Gusts of wind blow the paper about but nobody seems to notice. Farmers look at the images of their own animals and the landscape they know so intimately, seeing themselves and fragments of their lives through the eyes of strangers.

Keith Brockie: "The rapport and visual communication with the local people seeing their own animals and birds being painted was very gratifying and helped them understand our being here."

Sculptor Jaap Deelder works in the open as he does most of the time, using sharp chisels to hack away at a bird emerging from a chunk of wood laid across his unprotected legs. Larry Barth, a different kind of sculptor, usually works in the barn which serves as an all-weather studio, but today he is out in the open, painting his sculptures. Village children watch him from a respectful distance, their eyes wandering from his face to his hands, fascinated by the realism that seems to grow from his fingers. Later they crowd closer, and small circles of light reflecting off Barth's wristwatch dance across their faces and the weathered planks of The Barn.

A week ago, the artists had been warily watched by villagers from behind their garden fences as they unloaded camping gear, folding easels and telescopes from the bus that had brought them to the village from Warsaw on a damp and windy Saturday morning. "...good, lively people strong in body, suspicious in mind" is how James Michener characterized the Polish peasant in his chronicle of two dynasties in northeastern Poland.[13] Small villlages such as Waniewo were too poor and too far off the beaten track to get any attention from the trickle of tourists allowed into the country. It was not until 1990 that the first groups of western bird watchers came into the village, the peasants finding it incomprehensible that anyone would take the trouble of travelling so far to see something so ordinary as their marsh.

"Their suspicion is closely linked with their bad experiences in the past," wrote Eugeniusz Sokol. "To the simple men and women of Waniewo every visitor speaking a foreign language is a 'German'; their experiences with Germans in the past have made them wary of all strangers. The villagers were afraid you artists would make fun of their simple lives, they were greatly surprised to find so much interest shown in their daily work and in everything ancient."

The artists were the main subject in village gossip and a welcome change from daily cares, something to look at and wonder about. The villagers wondered about one man from the group in particular: the bearded man who went around barefoot. They asked Eugeniusz about the Norwegian Jon Fjeldså, wanting to know why a man from a rich western country couldn't afford a pair of shoes.

196) Ad Cameron: 'Waniewo' - watercolour 13 x 40 cms.
- Looking south towards the artists' camp and Narew marsh. A large part of the group of artists put up their tents behind Mayor Sokol's house, between Waniewo village and the Narew marsh. Despite the cold days at the outset and the generally cool nights throughout the stay, accounting for the absence of mosquitoes, camping out was agreeable. Once bedded down in a sleeping bag the sounds of birds in the marsh intruded - even in one's dreams. Keith Brockie: "Living in a tent lets one experience the night atmosphere. The memory of the nightly chorus still haunts me. The fluting call of the thrush nightingale, deep resounding booms from the bitterns, harsh barn owl calls and the croaking of frogs."

197

197) Ad Cameron.

198

Eugeniusz Sokol: "I never could have dreamt of so many unusual people visiting our village; you see, to me an artist is a very special person who feels and sees more than other humans and conveys this through his work. We experienced art on our own premises, saw it develop and were able to discuss the work at hand with the artist. I was positively surprised at how sensitive and understanding these foreigners were to me - they took their time to explain things which to me were new and interesting, but very ordinary to them."

Waniewo, and all the other villages in the area presented a delightful melange of farm life and wildlife, causing Larry Barth to comment: "Where I come from nature gets more interesting the further out one gets. The likelihood of seeing interesting and artistically stimulating images increases as you walk away from settlement - Waniewo was just the opposite: images came to me faster and faster *in* town."

John Busby: "My work shows the attitude of a perfect stranger seeing the village for the first time and trying to relate it to other experiences. There was so much not to miss out on it was difficult to narrow the choices to things which seemed to mean more to me."

"The problem of suitable subject matter," said Lawrence McQueen, "was that there was so much of it. I was pulled in many directions: by various aspects of the landscape, by the rich diversity of wildlife and by new bird species, by the villages and their people - and I wanted to spend time with other artists. Then there was the bus to take us to other universes."

SKETCHING IN THE FIELD

An artist generally needs time to understand a particular landscape - days, weeks, months before he can determine what is essential, years may pass before he or she is tuned in enough to be able to notice subtle shifts within the whole, let alone assess their meaning.

Time is essential. Time to wander, or to sit down somewhere - time to wait for something to happen. Often nothing does. You wait, and as you wait an awareness of your surroundings grows. Sounds seep in - the matchbox-rattle of magpies and from far away the call of a crane. Close by there are sounds that drown all other sounds. They seem to stress approaching dusk: the dry scraping of a twig against bark and a cascade of noise when you rise, knee-caps popping. The stool creaks in protest as you sink back.

If anything does take place, it often is unspectacular. The animal you were hoping to see shows itself as a mere blur and you are forced to reconstrue the fleeting image in your mind. Drawing helps, but the movement of the pencil across paper obliterates all other sounds. You hardly notice - the encounter (can it be called that?) and its reconstruction have become all-important.

Alan Johnston is squatting in the reeds, the movement of his head gives him away as he sketches birds I cannot see. He appears to be bowing in reverence to the telescope in front of him, unaware of my presence. On the sloping field behind him lapwings and redshanks cast angular shadows on the short grass, long-limbed and colourful godwits stand with beaks half-opened to get rid of excess body heat. A passing hooded crow spurs them into action and they rise in unison on powerful wingbeats, circling and calling as the crow is divebombed by lapwings when passing through their territories. Alan moves his head slightly, an acknowledgement of the passing event.

Alan Johnston:"I believe that the direct response to the field situation gives a quality to the work that is impossible to achieve in the studio."

It is a quality which has its price - field sketching is a time-consuming process and not always productive. Much time is spent just observing, drawing restricted to fits and starts. With these first lines the artist gropes for the complexities of form and volume, trying to analyse light and shade, and trying to see parts of the background in relation to the animal, one small piece in relation to the whole.

"Drawing," wrote John Busby in *Drawing Birds* "is like the unravelling of a mystery - a search for the true nature and meaning of an object."[14]

David Daly: "The only way I can paint is from direct observation, I need field studies for inspiration. Therefore I do many sketches from different angles, trying to understand it as a whole. Often the 'bits and pieces' in my sketchbook may seem incomprehensible to others, but to me they are the parts of a jigsaw that make up the final image."

199

198) *Bruce Pearson. Photo: Keith Brockie.* 199) *Andrew Halsen.* 200) *Robert Greenhalf, Waniewo.* 201) *Lawrence McQueen.*

200

201

Understanding is the ultimate goal. Provoked by the mystery of wild animals, roused by a wish to understand what is seen and felt, the artist needs the fragmentary sketches, they are vital in putting thought in order, vital in the search for what is essential.

The wariness and mobility of wild animals, an expression of their life force, pose great difficulties, forcing the artist to cope as best as he can under conditions which at times can be pleasant, or unfavourable to the extreme.

Most wildlife artists use optical aids such as binoculars and telescopes because it brings them up close to an animal without intruding on its natural behaviour, and quite a few artists use cameras and long lenses, amassing a great variety of images and information in a relatively short span of time. Those who criticize these 'recent' developments, forget that artists have used optical appliances to their advantage ever since the spread of the camera obscura, the precursor to the camera, in the 16th cemtury.

But when drawing animals on the spot a way has to be found of retaining what was seen, after the subject has changed position or moved away. The solution lies in the artist's ability to 'fix' in his mind the shape or movement of a subject, even if only for a short while. It is an ability which can be developed through practice - in the field.

Keith Brockie: "I enjoy sketching in the wild above all; the essence being able to bring life to sketches through personal experience. The intense focus of mind, eye and hand when sketching a subject which might depart at any moment is addictive, and transports me temporarily onto a different plane."

Elation, after having shared a moment of the life of another being, or frustration, from hours that have passed and pages that were filled but in which life seems so lacking. Time is never wasted though, for observation may result in something less tangible than a successful sketch, yet far more valuable: the artist has been filling in blank spots in his mind, storing information which some day may lead to the understanding he seeks.

Robert Greenhalf: "I usually start and complete my paintings in one go in the field, finding that work produced in this way has a spontaneity, born out of necessity to work quickly and instinctively. My studio work never seems to have the same life or authenticity - the temptation is to consider too deeply and to fiddle."

"Fieldwork is the only means to original and authentic portrayal of wildlife," says John Busby "at the same time many of the problems of communication are solved by compositional decisions in the studio."

When developing paintings from field observations an artist needs at least some sort of mental image of what he wants to achieve; the image can be precise, based on a specific field sketch or it can be vague, the artist having only a notion of the direction he wants to take.The image may change, evolving through various studies or through successive stages of the painting at hand. What is often lost in the process is the excitement felt at the moment of discovery, a feeling somehow conveyed by the immediacy and incompleteness of a sketch - its strongest charm.

Sometimes a sketch conveys an intensely experienced moment, making tangible the tension between observer and subject. If this is the case it can stand on its own, but generally a sketch is no more than a jotting in the prospect of an image more complete. This sequel, produced either in the field or in the studio, must be considered a failure if it doesn't add to the sketch, if other aspects which also are closely linked to observation fail to materialize.

Robert Bateman: "I think an artist should be completely open to ideas and inspiration the whole time. It gets a little risky at times if you've invested hundreds of hours in a picture, to take a chance near the end, (…) to be totally ruthless with a painting at any stage. I'm prepared to take these chances partly because I always have the confidence that I can get back something I've already achieved. For me it has to be exactly the way I want it, or I'd rather not have it all."[15]

I never got round to many things, and others expressed the same regret; ideas barely developed, ideas forgotten, or their importance reduced by time and distance. A mass of sketches never taken beyond the initial stage.

I never said goodbye to the skinny little girl in Sieburczyn who stood in the rain as I tried to finish an oil sketch, her large, solemn eyes following every move I made. She was young and shy and wore shoes that were a few sizes too big. The future of Poland, in outsize shoes.

Travelling back to Waniewo, staring at the landscape framed by the bus window, the horizon moves up and down, the fields of sprouting barley an extended blur of green. My eyes lock on haystacks, on rooks flocking above a colony in transparent trees and then on a field freshly ploughed, dark and damp like an open wound. The cooling colours are set off against a sky turning pink, the greens becoming phosphorescent, giving off the light they have absorbed during the day.

As dusk slides between us and the landscape the sky blushes to violet, then darkens to indigo and we sit looking at reflections of ourselves.

"I hope the landscape won't change; with my work I try to contribute at least a little to its conservation. That is all I can do," writes Charles Donker.

203

202

204

205

202) *Alan Johnston: 'Campsite flowers' - pencil and watercolour 42 x 30 cms.*
- Studies of Lady's smock, dandelion, ant, lace-fly and fly. Lady's smock, also known as cuckoo flower because its time of flowering coincides with the arrival of this bird, is a common plant found in hay meadows and along ditches, the Latin name *pratensis* meaning 'living in the meadow'. In marsh areas a variety occurs which is larger, the flowers whiter in colour and larger.

203) *Bruce Pearson: 'Artist's camp, Waniewo' - mixed media 40 x 57 cms.*

204) *Alan Johnston: 'Campsite frog (agile frog - detail)' - watercolour 32 x 30 cms.*

205) *Andrew Haslen: 'Hare among dandelions' - lino cut 16 x 20 cms.*

206) *Denis Clavreul: 'Robert Bateman drawing in the barn' - pencil 30 x 41 cms.*

206

207

"Field sketching is a wonderful activity for those who have the taste and talent for it. It is even quite nice for those who don't. Sitting out in nature, the wind blowing in your hair, the scents of nature in your nostrils, the sounds in your ears and the fleeting, dynamic sights in your eyes is good for the soul no matter who you are. Forcing yourself to look and really *see* amplifies the sense of being alive and 'tuned in'.

I came here to enjoy the landscape for my own observation and art, and to see things that have a human heritage as well as a natural heritage. I had heard that this district still has traditional ways and has not been overwhelmed by a lot of 20th century influences. The 20th century adds up to more bad than good points for the future of the world. If we're going to have a sustainable future we're going to have to start following more traditional ways that have worked for many, many centuries. This area in Poland is one of the remnants where people still follow traditional ways. I hope we can draw the attention of the world into protecting this area. We must show people that this is a precious heritage, if we don't do anything it surely will be destroyed."

- *Robert Bateman (Canada)*

208

209

207) *Robert Bateman: 'Old shed' - pen and ink 11 x 28 cms.*
208) *Denis Clavreul: 'Cockerel and hen' - pencil and watercolour 30 x 41 cms.*
209) *Keith Brockie: 'The dust bath' - watercolour 38 x 51 cms.*
   - "Normally I sketch a subject from several angles so as to improve on each continuously as it moves around. I initially sketch the rough outline and form as quickly as I can, adding as much detail as possible while the subject stays nearby."[16]

210

212

211

162

213

214

210) *John Busby: 'Pigs' - watercolour 34 x 50 cms.*

211) *Robin D'Arcy Shillcock: 'Waniewo fence' - pencil and watercolour*
    14 x 19 cms.

212) *Else Behring: 'Calves' - pencil 21 x 29 cms.*
    - "It is very difficult to draw the jumping calves but after a while
    they lie down in the soft grass and sleep. I am absorbed in drawing,
    the sun warms me, life is full of joy - although my hand does not
    always succeed in truly capturing the images before me."

213) *Robin D'Arcy Shillcock: 'Balbina' - pencil 30 x 42 cms.*
    - "Some animals enjoyed our presence, despite our analysing stares;
    I'm pretty sure that Balbina, the local broken-winged goose, enjoyed
    my presence as I trailed behind her around all the farmyards -
    whilst she drank and washed in buckets of freshly drawn water I
    peered into barns where hay lay piled high, and while I was treated
    to small tumblers of vodka she chased away sparrows collecting
    chicken feathers for lining their little nests."

214) *Siegfried Woldhek: 'Artist Jon Feldså at work' - watercolour 25 x 20 cms.*

216

215

164

215) *Denis Clavreul: 'Waniewo sketches' - pencil and watercolour 30 x 41 cms.*
216) *Jon Fjeldså: 'The Barn and swallow' - watercolour 28 x 21 cms.*
217) *Robin D'Arcy Shillcock: 'Vegetable Garden, Sieburczyn' - oil on panel*
     24 x 30 cms.
218) *Dag Peterson: 'Oak, Waniewo' - pencil 27 x 36 cms.*

219

221

220

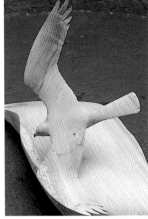

222

223

THE BARN

The tables in The Barn were a constant disarray of sketchbooks, paintboxes, water bottles, binoculars and fieldguides - and steaming cups of coffee and packed lunches. Some came in at the end of a day's painting to finish their outdoor studies, others, like Piet Eggen, worked on plants taken from the dark water of the marsh, or fish kept in watertanks. Live lizards, frogs and insects were brought in, quickly drawn and released again. There were eggshells, snails, plants and, occasionally a dead bird. A yellow wagtail was found, a whinchat and a beautifully marked nightjar, soft and with large, dark eyes and a large beak for catching insects in flight. The beak, when opened, showed a pink lining - a soft bed for insects to die in.

219) *Ad Cameron: 'Sand lizard studies' - pen drawing with watercolour 24 x 30 cms.*
    - In spring the male lizard has bright green flanks. The pattern on the back marks each individual like the fingerprints of a human hand.

220) *Jon Fjeldså: 'Dead yellow wagtail' - watercolour 23 x 31 cms.*

221) *Dag Peterson: 'Nightjar' - lithograph 13 x 18 cms.*

222-223) *Jaap Deelder: 'Montague's harrier' - red oak 45 x 75 cms.*

225

226

227

224) *Jaap Deelder: 'Group of black terns' - coromandel ebony, length ca. 22 cms.*
   - "I had set my mind to working on a limited number of species but
   during my stay in Poland I fell in love with the graceful Montague's
   harrier and the spotted eagle. The stork was another bird which
   impressed me, but I don't think I can capture its beauty in wood.
   I talked a lot with carver Larry Barth and was impressed by his
   knowledge and craftmanship in modelling. As an experiment I
   painted one of my sculptures but you can hardly call this 'influence'
   - though I admire his work I will never follow the direction. Wood
   is too important for me and I find it exciting to show the natural
   material."
225) *Jaap Deelder: 'Lesser spotted eagle' - elm, height 50 cms.*
226-227) *Larry Barth: 'Yellow wagtail' - polyform and acrylic,
   height 36 cms.*

229

228

230

231

228-229) *Larry Barth: 'Whinchat' - polyform and acrylic, height 56.5 cms.*
230) *Larry Barth: 'Yellow wagtail' - polyform and acrylic, height 40 cms.*
231) *Larry Barth: 'Nightjar' - polyform and acrylic, length 25 cms.*

- Barth studies his subject in the field, making small sketches and if dead specimens are at hand he will do detailed studies of these as well. Both yellow wagtail and whinchat were brought in dead, but fresh.

After modelling the bird in a sculpturing clay of chemical compound, he paints the models - the most time-consuming part of the process requiring utmost concentration. This meticulously painted clay model generally serves as a preliminary - but exhaustive - study for the very detailed carvings in wood. "I like to know where I'm going, I do not want any surprises," he says.

Scarlet Robin   Warrenup   Kim Atkinson

232

233

172

234

232) *Kim Atkinson: 'Scarlet rosefinch in the orchard behind The Barn' -
    charcoal and watercolour 36.5 x 30 cms.*
233) *Tomasz Cofta: 'Collared flycatcher (female)' - colour pencil 18 x 20 cms.*
234) *Denis Clavreul: 'Kim Atkinson drawing from a canoe (detail)' - pencil
    30 x 41 cms.*
235) *Kim Atkinson: 'Dragonroot' - watercolour 29 x 42 cms.*

235

236

237

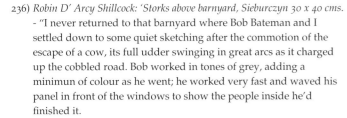

236) *Robin D' Arcy Shillcock: 'Storks above barnyard, Sieburczyn 30 x 40 cms.*
- "I never returned to that barnyard where Bob Bateman and I
settled down to some quiet sketching after the commotion of the
escape of a cow, its full udder swinging in great arcs as it charged
up the cobbled road. Bob worked in tones of grey, adding a
minimun of colour as he went; he worked very fast and waved his
panel in front of the windows to show the people inside he'd
finished it.
Seeing his painting reproduced somewhere I thought: that's not
how I remember it. In my imagination everything had a shell-like
gleam and clarity."
237) *Siegfried Woldhek: 'Waniewo' - watercolour 21 x 29 cms.*
238) *Robert Bateman: 'Well and storks, Sieburczyn' - acrylic on board*
    30 x 19 cms.

THE FUTURE

"Change is unavoidable, but we want progress to adjust to what nature has to offer, and we want a human existence that will not cause irreversible damage to the environment . The needs of man and the needs of nature should exist as a unity."
- Krzysztof Wolfram

"The most overwhelming feeling I have," wrote artist Dave Daly after returning to his home near Cork in Ireland, "is of having witnessed something unique - something I may never see again. Were we among the pioneers of change, will our focus of attention on that primeval landscape change its fate? "

The fate of the Biebrza depends on a future which is as complex as the river itself, but above all its fate depends on choices made in favour of its protection.

Tourism will have an important part to play in the future of the Biebrza, for as rumour spreads of its natural riches, people who are hungry for a taste of wilderness will go there to watch birds, and to hunt elk, roe deer and boar. They will want to travel the river in their lightweight canoes, and fish its rich waters as they drift. They will want to enter the remote reaches of the marsh.

Tourism may be good or bad, depending on your point of view. The money it brings will help improve the livelihood of the local population, which is good. Too many holidaymakers will most certainly cause disturbance in the landscape and a disruption of the slow pace of village life. That's bad.

The scenario of change proposed by Krzysztof Wolfram of The Office of the Green Lungs of Poland Agreement, foresees the influx of tourists and the changes they will bring. He pleads for an organised form of tourism and a carefully controlled and well-balanced development of industry, agriculture and forestry in northeastern Poland, one of the poorest regions in the country. It is an ambitious plan in both vision and scope, it stipulates that progress must not be allowed to inflict irreversible damage to ecologically valuable areas - the compilers understood that the region's greatest asset is its variety of undisturbed natural habitat. Their keyword is *sustainable* development, a progress which the environment can endure.

This does not mean that the old conceptions of marshland, seeing it as 'unproductive wasteland', have disappeared. Drainage schemes, though temporarily shelved and gahering dust, still exist. Presented when agriculture becomes profitable again, they are sure to win the votes of farmers who believe in a future with larger farms, big machines and lots of fertilizer as a warrant for huge turnovers.

Conservation, like painting, isn't a matter of mathematics. Going one step forwards in one area often means taking two backwards in another, a process of gradual development and often infuriatingly slow progress. What is lost in painting can - in most cases - be regained, that is part of the artist's craft. But what is lost in nature cannot be regained, nor rebuilt. In western countries a hard lesson is being learned, and an expensive attempt made to retrieve what was squandered within the life span of barely two generations. The lesson is: don't do what we did, don't wait until it is too late.

Robert Bateman: "...the best things in life are not free anymore. They used to be free. Clean air, clean water, the song of a bird used to be free in the good old days. They are not free anymore; they are expensive. But they are an awful lot cheaper now than they will be by the year 2000. We had better start spending money on clean air, clean water and the song of the birds and all that entails now, while it is cheap, while it is a bargain - can you imagine what our children are going to have to spend for that kind of thing?"[17]

Since focusing attention on Poland in 1990 WWF International has recognised that the Biebrza wetland is without parallel in the west and that its preservation will also depend on the attitude of local farmers who dream of better incomes from modern farming methods. Farmers must be made aware of the importance of the marshes, of the delicate balance of interdependent life forms - a balance so easily upset by radical changes in farming. Alternatives must be found, involving farmers in park management and compensating them for applying traditional ways of working the land and for mowing the hay meadows in the marsh by hand.

Andrew Haslen: " Groups like ours will eventually play a part in changing things, but I believe the long term survival of the marshes is linked very strongly to the people on its banks."

Jon Fjeldså: "Over the years I have become increasingly aware of the fact that local people should not be seen as an obstacle but as the best opportunity for conservation. The main problem is communication, to local people - who ask what is nature good for? - about the value of nature, and to politicians about the importance of incorporating environmental concerns into their plans for development and economic theories."

239) *John Busby: 'Early mist, Waniewo' - oil on canvas 61 x 91 cms.*
- "The marshes under a white shroud in early morning. The only movement that of a man taking his cows for a drink, the only sounds the unmuffled calls of bittern, great reed warblers and black terns."

WORLD WIDE FUND FOR NATURE (WWF)

In 1990 WWF International, aware of the variety and extent of pristine habitats in the former communist countries, turned its attention to Eastern Europe. Understanding that problems regarding conservation are affected by political, economic and social developments, WWF tries to make clear to western countries that every penny spent on environmental protection in former communist countries will be of benefit to all of Europe. In the east WWF plays an advisory role to conservation bodies and financially supports a wide variety of activities aimed at wetland protection, ecological farming, specialised forms of tourism and reduction of pollution.

In close cooperation with the Polish government and regional protection societies and with funds from the Dutch government, WWF has initially singled out two projects of major importance to the Biebrza wetlands: the foundation of the Biebrza National Park and the financial support of farms converting to ecological farming.

Funds for a management and investment plan for the National Park were raised by WWF. Presented in 1992 the plan proposes a reserve that will cover the Biebrza River from source to its confluence with the Narew, making it the largest National Park in Poland.

The five year plan, recquiring an investment upwards of US $ 5 million, entails the erection of a new park administration centre, a re-naturalization of the middle basin, instalment of waste and sewage treatment plants, the development of an educational programme and monitoring studies on flora and fauna. Four or five farms will serve as model farms - the most effective way to increase ecological awareness and to convince farmers of better methods. The formal inauguration of the Biebrza National Park, by H.R.H.Prince Bernhard of the Netherlands, is planned for May 1994.

(For address see List of Organisations on page 190)

In 1984, during communist rule, the Biebrza marshes were designated a Landscape Park but it meant very little in the way of real protection. Since then pressure from WWF and Polish conservation bodies has resulted in a national consensus on the foundation of a National Park, and in the presentation of a detailed management and investment plan.

BIEBRZA NATIONAL PARK

The National Park will consist of 59,000 ha surrounded by a bufferzone of another 89,000 ha, making it the largest reserve in Poland. A staff of 138 will run the park from the information centre in the town of Osowiec.

Re-naturalization of the partly drained areas in the middle basin will be necessary to preserve the natural development and diversity of flora and fauna communities. It will be achieved by gradually closing down the Woznawiejski and Rudzki canals, causing the ground water to rise to a natural level.

To protect the National Park against pollution washed out from sewage and drainage canals small treatment plants will have to be installed in villages or near isolated homesteads in the marshes.

Over the past twenty years extensive scientific research has been carried out in the Biebrza Valley but gaps still remain which hinder the overall understanding of its ecology. Extensive research of flora and fauna will have to be carried out and aerial and satellite photography used for data on the extent of annual inundations. Much needs to be done - a national park built from scratch!

Krzysztof Wolfram: "For many of us the calling of cranes during their mating dance, the clappering of storks and the splashing of beaver tails on quiet backwaters are echoes from our past. For these, for the preservation of habitat and, ultimately, for the survival of the natural order of the Biebrza and Upper Narew Valley we have been fighting for years."

Victoria Crowe: "Looking back, I think the quality most important to me was the slow unfolding of an understanding of the place, an understanding which could only have been achieved by living there. I made friends with one of the girls of a Polish family living just opposite 'our' house - I felt it was important to contact the young people as they have the future of the marshes in their hands. In a letter Malgorzat Idzikowska thanks me for taking an interest in 'simple people such as we', it is a lovely correspondence and my whole family has already been invited back to stay in that tiny wooden house with them - six children, her parents and her granny."

"There's an innocence and fondness which goes hand in hand with that non-materialistic life style - I'm not idealising poverty by any means, but I appreciate the way simple things are valued so much."

"In a way I think that this communication we are all

241

GREEN LUNGS OF POLAND (GLP)

An answer to the problems of northeastern Poland can be found in the Green Lungs of Poland Agreement, formulated in 1983 by Krzysztof Wolfram and developed by Stefan Koslowski, environmental expert of Solidarity, member of parliament and former Minister of Environmental Protection.
The plan is based on a sustainable economical development which is *integrated* with the natural character of the GLP region which covers an area of 50,000 sq. kms., roughly the triangle between Warsaw in the south, Gdansk on the Baltic coast and the borders with Russia and Lithuania. The area contains habitat of international ecological importance such as the Bialowieza Forest, which is on the UNESCO List of World Human Heritage as a biosphere reserve, the Mazurian Lakes, the Biebrza Valley and eighteen other areas which will be linked to form a 'green' belt in which there will be place for both man and wildlife.
The Office of the Green Lungs of Poland Agreement, a unit of the National Foundation for Environmental Protection (NFEP), supports a number of activities which will help protect the diversity in the Biebrza area, such as stimulating local farmers to produce health foods, the construction of small sewage treatment plants in villages along the Biebrza and the promotion of unleaded petrol use.

The GLP plan is supported by the Ministry of Natural Resources, Environmental Preservation and Forestry and WWF International. The idea has already spread beyond the borders of Poland: in early 1992 the authorities of Poland, Russia, Byelorussia, Lithuania, Latvia and Ukraine signed a declaration of intent for a joint plan based on sustainable development and environmental protection - a possible 'Green Lungs of Europe'.

(For address see 'List of Organisations' on page 190)

trying to achieve through painting comes very close in this instance; a breaking down of barriers, a respect for our differing life styles, *these* are the building blocks that have to be in place before we can 'change the world', before we can make people aware of our message about the Biebrza Marshes."

240) *Charles Donker: 'Stork' - pen and ink 12 x 20 cms.*
241) *Bruce Pearson: 'Barnyard' - mixed media 40 x 50 cms.*

242

243

242) *Robert Bateman: 'Barnyard with dead rook (field study)' - acrylic on board 14.5 x 40 cms.*
    - "I enjoy painting man-made and domestic objects and buildings when they show some wear and age and the surfaces suggest the accumulation of events over the years."[18]
243) *Keith Brockie: 'Stork on nest' - watercolour 38 x 55 cms.*
244) *Robert Bateman: 'Barnyard with dead rook' - acrylic on board 61 x 91 cms.*

Robert Bateman 1993 ©

244

245

246

247

245) *Victoria Crowe: 'Wooden house' - watercolour 25 x 35 cms.*
246) *Denis Clavreul: 'Ortolan bunting (detail)' - pencil and watercolour*
   30 x 41 cms.
247) *Larry McQueen: 'Shadow of stork nest, Waniewo' - watercolour*
   28 x 40 cms.
   - "Studies for this painting were done at the end of our stay, after I
   noticed the cast shadows of the storks and their nest on the side of
   the barn. Nesting storks have become the symbol of the Biebrza
   Valley for us, and these shadows are symbolic of our farewell to
   them, to Waniewo, to the Biebrza, and to Poland.
   In a larger sense, these shadows and the nearby cemetery of
   Waniewo in the composition are symbolic of impending doom, as
   the stork continues to decline in its once broad range. It could
   become extinct in Poland, even become extinct as a species. This
   shadow could symbolize the illusion that remains in the face of
   modern development; the illusion of a once beautiful land with
   beautiful species."

248

248) *Vadim Gorbatov: 'Black stork over the lower basin - watercolour 41 x 31 cms.*

249) *Bruce Pearson: 'Biebrza marsh from Burzyn' - mixed media 21 x 30 cms.*

Biebrza Marshes from Bareya.
10/may/92.

Bruno Pearson

249

250

250) *Peter Partington: 'Biebrza landscape' - watercolour 15 x 37 cms.*
251) *Vadim Gorbatov: 'Wolf family' - watercolour 70 x 47 cms.*
- Bruce Pearson: "As if to emphasize the ancient nature of this wilderness there are two family parties of wolves surviving in the remotest part of the valley. To see those in the wild would be thrilling indeed, but just knowing that they are there, in the heart of Europe, is satisfaction enough."

Artist's biographies

PHOTO: FRED HAZELHOFF

PHOTO: FRED HAZELHOFF

THE ARTISTS

First row, from left to right: David Daly, Kim Atkinson, Keith Brockie, Robert Greenhalf, Jaap Deelder, Jon Fjeldså, Denis Clavreul, Chris Rose, Andrew Haslen, Michael Warren, Siegfried Woldhek, Bruce Pearson, Victoria Crowe, Piet Eggen, Greg Septon, Ad Cameron.
Second row: Jean Chevallier, Robin D'Arcy Shillcock, Dag Peterson, Tomasz Cofta, Vadim Gorbatov, Else Behring, Hans Geuze, LarryBarth, Darren Rees, Robert Bateman, John Busby, Lawrence McQueen, Peter Partington, Alan Johnston and Charles Donker.

- "I think an enormous camaraderie built up as the meeting progressed. Whilst we are all solitary by nature, and at first were inhibited - we gained enormous strength by realising we had so many brothers. This surely will help us all help the natural world in turn."
- Peter Partington (England)

(* means artist took part in the international meeting on the Dutch barrier island Schiermonnikoog in 1990)

KIM ATKINSON

- Born in 1964 in Somerset, England. Studied at Falmouth School of Art, The Cheltenham School of Art and the Royal College of Art in London. She lives on Bardsey Island, off the Welsh coast, and works as a painter, printmaker and on the island's only farm.

LARRY BARTH

- Born in 1957 in the USA. Studied illustration at the Carnegie-Mellon University, Pittsburgh. Has made decorative wildfowl carvings since he was fourteen. In 1991 he was honoured as 'master wildlife artist' by LYWAM, USA.
- He lives in Stahlstown, USA.

ROBERT BATEMAN

- Born in Toronto, Canada in 1930. Studied geography and art at the University of Toronto. His art developed from naturalism through modernist styles to his present realistic style which is influenced by Andrew Wyeth. Travels the world widely in search of subject matter for paintings which reflect his dedication to the preservation of nature's diversity. His concern was put forward in *The best things in life are not free anymore (Wildlife Art News, 1990)*. Several books on his art have appeared.
- Bateman was honoured by Canada in 1984 as Officer of the Order of Canada, the country's highest civilian award, and he bears numerous honorary doctorates and international awards.
- He resides on the Pacific coast of Canada.

ELSE BEHRING

- Born in 1935. Studied graphic design and now works as an exhibition designer for the Zoological Museum in Copenhagen, designing educational material explaining ecology and conservation. She has illustrated several books, including children's books on wildlife.
- She resides in Copenhagen, Denmark.

KEITH BROCKIE *

- Born in Haddington, Scotland in 1955. Studied illustration and printmaking at Duncan of Jordanstone College of Art, Dundee. He has travelled from Yemen to the Arctic in search of birds as both bird-ringer as artist. He has illustrated numerous bird books, is the author of three books on Scottish wildlife and is now working on his fourth.
- He lives near Invergowrie in Scotland.

JOHN BUSBY *

- Born in 1928 in Bradford, England. Studied at Leeds and Edinburgh Colleges of Art and taught drawing and painting at Edinburgh College of Art for over thirty years. He makes large-scale landscape and abstract paintings and is a prolific illustrator of books on wildlife. He wrote the monograph on the art of Eric Ennion, by whom he was influenced, and the comprehensive *Drawing Birds - a RSPB guide. (Helm 1986)*
He resides in Ormiston, on the Firth of Forth coast of Scotland.

AD CAMERON *

- Born in 1939, Vlissingen, the Netherlands. Studied illustration at the Royal Academy in The Hague. Cameron worked as an advertising artist before becoming a free-lance illustrator in the late 70's, specialising in birds and related subjects. He has illustrated several bird books, including *Owls of the Northern Hemisphere*.
- He lives in Wierum on the Dutch Wadden Sea coast.

JEAN CHEVALLIER

- Born in Boulogne-Bilancourt, France in 1961. Self-taught artist. After studying biology he turned to illustration and printmaking, specialising in nature subjects of France and North Africa.
- He resides in Fresnes, France.

DENIS CLAVREUL *

- Born in 1955 in France. Studied biology at the University of Rennes. Clavreul is a self-taught artist, developing as an illustrator after leaving university in 1985. He has illustrated numerous magazines and books on nature for both adults and children.
- He resides in Nantes, France.

TOMASZ COFTA

- Born in 1956 in Gdansk. Works as a scientist on songbird migration along the Baltic Sea coast. He has published articles in Polish and Swedish ornithological journals and is currently working on the illustrations for a handbook on Polish birds.
- He resides in Gdansk, Poland.

VICTORIA CROWE

- Born in 1945, Kingston-on-Thames, England. Studied at the Kingston and Royal Colleges of Art in London. She teaches part-time at the Edinburgh College of Art and works as a landscape and portrait painter, receiving portrait commissions from, among others, the National Portrait Gallery in London, Edinburgh University and The National Trust for Scotland.
- She resides in West Linton, The Borders, Scotland.

DAVID DALY

- Born in 1956, Ireland. Daly specializes in bird painting and has shown his work in Ireland.
- He resides in Wexford, in Ireland.

JAAP DEELDER *

- Born in 1952 on the Dutch barrier island of Terschelling. Works as a teacher for retarded children. Deelder is a self-taught woodcarver with a preference for a natural finish on his sculptures.
- He lives in Noordwijk, the Netherlands.

CHARLES DONKER *

- Born in 1940 in Utrecht, the Netherlands. Studied monumental design at the Academy for Art and Design in 's-Hertogenbosch. Turned to monochrome printmaking in the 1960's and now works as a printmaker and watercolour painter. A book of his art was published in 1977.
- He lives in Utrecht, the Netherlands.

PIET EGGEN

- Born in 1949 in Klimmen, the Netherlands. Studied at the Art Academy of Maastricht. He works as a free-lance illustrator, does all kinds of nature related subjects for nature magazines and advertising. He has a preference for insects and fish.
- He resides in Dedemsvaart, the Netherlands, where he runs a gallery specializing in art inspired by nature.

JON FJELDSÅ

- Born in 1942 in Bodø, Norway. Studied zoology in Bergen, Norway. He now lives in Copenhagen and is head of the zoological department of the Zoological Museum. He has travelled widely in Africa, Asia and South America to conduct zoological fieldwork and now works on theoretical questions relevant to conservation. He has published numerous scientific papers and is author of the *Guide to the Young of European Precocial Birds*. His artwork consists mainly of illustrations for scientific papers and books linked to conservation, like guides and educational books.

HANS J. GEUZE *

- Born in 1936 in Bergen op Zoom, the Netherlands. Studied biology at the Free University in Amsterdam. Working as a professor of cell biology at the University of Utrecht leaves him little time to paint and travel in search of birds. He specialises in watercolour painting.
- Hans Geuze is President of Artists for Nature Foundation.
- He lives in Kockengen, the Netherlands

VADIM GORBATOV *

- Born in 1940 in Moscow, Russia. Studied at the Academy of Art, Industrial Design and Applied Arts in Moscow. Worked as an illustrator for Soviet Television, later becoming head of the Television Nature Deptartment. He has travelled all over the former Soviet Union to study wildlife, including many of the larger mammals. Gorbatov now works as a free-lance illustrator and has illustrated several books on wildlife.
- He lives in Moscow, Russia.

ROBERT GREENHALF

- Born in England in 1950. Studied at Eastbourne and Maidstone Art Colleges. Having worked mainly as a printmaker for many years he has now turned to watercolour painting, with birds and their environment as his main subject.
- He lives in Rye in England.

ANDREW HASLEN *

- Born in 1953 in England. Works as a painter of wildlife and domestic animals and runs the Wildlife Art Gallery in Lavenham.
- He resides in Scobury, Fngland.

FRED HAZELHOFF

- Born in 1925, in The Hague in the Netherlands. Studied photography and graphic design at the Royal Academy of Arts in The Hague. He worked as art director for a publishing company, as editor of a photography magazine and as a teacher at the Academy of Fine Arts in Enschede and Rotterdam. He now works as a free-lance photographer, travelling to four continents in search of subject matter. His work has been published in numerous magazines and he is the author of six books on wildlife.
- He resides in Zelhem in the Netherlands.

ALAN F. JOHNSTON *

- Born in 1959, in Zürich, Switzerland. Studied wildlife illustration at Dyfed College of Art in Wales. Worked as a nature warden, and as a taxidermist and illustrator for natural history museums in Glasgow and Luxemburg. He works as a free-lance illustrator and is the author of a book on Luxemburg wildlife.
- He resides in Asselborn, Luxemburg.

LAWRENCE B. MCQUEEN

- Born in 1936, USA. Studied biology at Bucknell University in Pennsylvania and Idaho State University, and art at the University of Oregon in Eugene. McQueen worked as a field biologist and as a staff illustrator at the Oregon State Museum of Anthropology. He now works as a free-lance illustrator and painter of birds and has published work in several handbooks on birds. He has invested years of work for an illustrated guide to the birds of Peru.
- McQueen resides in Eugene, Oregon, USA.

PETER PARTINGTON

- Born in 1941 in Cambridge, England. Studied art at Bournemouth and Hornsey Colleges of Art. He taught painting full time for almost twenty years. Starting out as an abstract painter Partington turned to wildlife and now works as a free-lance artist, illustrator and printmaker and is the author of *Birds in Watercolour*.
- He lives in Gravesend, in England.

BRUCE PEARSON

- Born in 1950, England. Studied Fine Art at the Leicester Polytechnic. Worked for the RSPB Film Unit before turning to art and illustration. He travels widely in search of subject matter, including the Antarctic. He has written and presented a television series on birds and their habitat and has followed birds on migration from the Arctic to Africa - both themes resulting in *An artist on Migration* and *Birdscape*.
- He resides in Great Gransden, England.

DAG PETERSON *

- Born in 1939 in Varberg, Sweden. Worked for the Swedish American Lines and, after following a written course of the Famous Artists Schools, as an advertising artist. He became a full-time bird painter in 1975. He was involved in the Eagle Owl Project in Sweden and breeds golden eagles in Fritsla, Sweden, where he lives.

DARREN REES*

- Born in 1961 in Andover, England. Studied mathematics at Southampton University, but turned to bird painting and illustation after a short spell of teaching. He has illustrated several bird books and a first major publication of his art is due in autumn 1993.
- He now resides in Boston, USA.

CHRIS ROSE

- Born in 19.. in Uganda. He works as a free-lance illustrator and painter specializing in birds. He illustrated a book on mountain birds and is now working on a monograph on wheatears and Malayan birds.
- He lives in Melrose, Scotland.

ROBIN D'ARCY SHILLCOCK*

- Born in 1953 in the Netherlands. Studied at the Academy of Fine Arts in Groningen, The Netherlands. He taught drawing and painting and worked as a plein air landscape painter before turning to wildlife. He has illustrated several books and has written and lectured on wildlife art and landscape painting.
- He resides in Groningen, the Netherlands.

MICHAEL WARREN *

- Born 1938, England. Studied at Wolverhampton College of Art. Worked as a designer before turning to bird painting in the early 70's. He designed a set of stamps for the Royal Post Office and conservation stamps for the Audubon Society. He published a book in 1984 called *Shorelines*.
- He resides in Nottinghamshire, England.

SIEGFRIED WOLDHEK*

- Born in 1951 in Emmen, the Netherlands. Studied biology at the Free University in Amsterdam. Woldhek is a self-taught artist specializing in cartoons for national Dutch newspapers. He is the former president of the Dutch Society for Bird Protection and current director of WWF-Holland.
- He resides in Zeist, the Netherlands.

WIKTOR WOLKOW

- Born in 1942 in Bialystok, Poland. He has worked almost exclusively in the Biebrza and Narew area for over thirty years, specializing in 'impressionistic' photography, using heavy grain, graphic effects and hand-held 500 and 1000 mm telephoto lenses. All elements of the marsh landscape are used as themes, e.g. birds, plough horses, haystacks, fences and the landscape itself, which he also photographed extensively from the air. He has exhibited his Biebrza studies and has produced a black and white book on the area called *Wolkow*.
- He resides in Suprasl, Poland.

Acknowledgements

Bibliography

"Biebrza: uniek veenmoeras in Polen" by A. Barendregt, J. de Smidt and M. Wassen (*Panda* May 1990).

"East Europe's Dark Dawn" by Jon Thompson (*National Geographic* vol. 179, no 6, June 1991).

Five Years Protection Plan of a National Park in Biebrza Valley, Poland by NFEP and WWF -WWF Project 3943 (1992).

Green Lungs of Poland , idea of protection, development strategy, pragmatics, by K. Wolfram, GLP Office (1992).

"Het Moerasecosysteem in Noordoost-Polen" by A. Barendregt and A. van Leeuwen (*Huid en Haar* no.1 1992).

Outline of a Regional Policy for the Eco-region "Green Lungs of Poland" by NFEP (1991).

Ptaki biebranskich bagien by G., S. and T. Klosowski (KSAT 1991).

PTOP Information Brochure.

List of organisations

ARTISTS FOR NATURE FOUNDATION (ANF)
Director Mr. Ysbrand Brouwers sr.
P.O. Box 1
7700 AA Dedemsvaart the Netherlands
Telephone: 05230 - 13571 Fax: 05230 - 16697

WORLD WIDE FUND FOR NATURE (WWF)
CH - 1196 Gland Switzerland
Telephone: 022 - 3649111 Fax: 022 - 3644238

GREEN LUNGS OF POLAND (GLP)
The Office of the Green Lungs of Poland Agreement
Director Mr. Krzysztof Wolfram
ul. Elektryczna 12
15 - 080 Bialystok Poland
Telephone/fax: 085 - 412105

NATIONAL FOUNDATION FOR ENVIRONMENTAL PROTECTION (NFEP)
Krzywickiego 9
02 - 078 Warsaw Poland
Telephone: 022 - 252127 Fax: 022 - 251428

THE NORTH-PODLASIE SOCIETY FOR BIRD PROTECTION (PTOP)
Chairman Mr. Przemyslaw Bielicki
P.O. Box 32
17 - 230 Bialowieza Poland
Telephone: 085 - 618202

BIRD SERVICE TOURIST AGENCY
Director Mr. Maciej Zimowski
ul. ks. Popieluszki 105
15 - 641 Bialystok Poland
Telephone/Fax: 085 - 616768

Notes:

Introduction

1: *Down the River* Victor Gollancz Ltd. 1987.
2: *Arctic Dreams* Bantam Books 1986.
3: *Poland* by James Michener, Corgi Books 1984.
4: 'East Europe's Dark Dawn' by Jon Thompson *National Geographic*, vol. 179, no. 6 1991.
5: see 4.
6: Ballantine Books 1991.

A farmers world

7: Eugeniusz Sokol, translator, boatman and guide working for Bird Service Tourist Agency and son of our host, the mayor of Waniewo.

Wildlife of the Narew

8: *The Painted Bird* Pocket Book 1971.
9: *A Silvery Tay* Dent 1988.

The biebrza valley

10: *Theodore Rousseau* by A.Terrasse, Henri Scrépel, 1976.
11: Victor Gollancz Ltd. 1987.

Through the eyes of strangers

12: *Theodore Rousseau* by A. Terrasse, Henri Scrépel, 1976.
13: *Poland* Corgi Books 1984.
14: Helm 1986.
15: *The World of Robert Bateman* by R. Derry. Madison Press Books 1984.
16: *A Silvery Tay* Dent 1988.

The future

17: *Wildlife Art News* March/April 1990.
18: *The World of Robert Bateman* by R. Derry, Madison Press Books 1985.

INDEX: FLORA AND FAUNA MENTIONED IN TEXT

BIRDS

Aquatic warbler *Acrocephalus paludicola*
Barn owl *Tyto alba*
Bittern *Botaurus stellaris*
Black-headed gull *Larus ridibundus*
Black stork *Ciconia nigra*
Black-tailed godwit *Limosa limosa*
Black tern *Chlidonias niger*
Bluethroat *Luscinia svecica*
Blue tit *Parus caeruleus*
Collared flycatcher *Ficedula albicollis*
Corncrake *Crex crex*
Crane *Grus grus*
Cuckoo *Cuculus canorus*
Eagle owl *Bubo bubo*
Garganey *Anas querquedula*
Golden oriole *Oriolus oriolus*
Goshawk *Accipiter gentilis*
Great snipe *Gallinago media*
Grebe *Podiceps spec*
Hobby *Falco subbuteo*
Hooded crow *Corvus corone cornix*
Hoopoe *Upupa epops*
Jackdaw *Corvus monedula*
Lapwing *Vanellus vanellus*
Lesser spotted eagle *Aquila pomarina*
Lesser whitethroat *Sylvia curruca*
Little bittern *Ixobrychus minutus*
Little crake *Porzana parva*
Little tern *Sterna albifrons*
Long-eared owl *Asio otus*
Magpie *Pica pica*
Mallard *Anas platyrhynchos*
Marsh harrier *Circus aeruginosus*
Montague's harrier *Circus pygargus*
Mute swan *Cygnus olor*
Nightjar *Caprimulgus europaeus*
Ortolan bunting *Emberiza hortulana*
Penduline tit *Remiz pendulinus*
Red-backed shrike *Lanius collurio*
Red-footed falcon *Falco vespertinus*
Redshank *Tringa totanus*
Reed bunting *Emberiza schoeniclus*
Rook *Corvus frugilegus*
Ruff *Philomachus pugnax*
Savi's warbler *Locustella luscinioides*
Scarlet rosefinch *Carpodacus erythrinus*
Short-eared owl *Asio flammeus*
Short-toed eagle *Circaetus gallicus*
Shoveler *Anas clypeata*
Snipe *Gallinago gallinago*
Spotted crake *Porzana porzana*
Spotted eagle *Aquila clanga*
Stork *Ciconia ciconia*

Swallow *Hirundo rustica*
Thrush nightingale *Luscinia luscinia*
Treecreeper *Certhia familiaris*
Tree sparrow *Passer montanus*
Water rail *Rallus aquaticus*
Wheatear *Oenanthe oenanthe*
Whinchat *Saxicola rubetra*
Whiskered tern *Chlidonias hybridus*
White-backed woodpecker *Dendrocopos leucotos*
White-fronted goose *Anser erythropus*
White-tailed or sea eagle *Haliaeetus albicilla*
White-winged black tern *Chlidonias leucopterus*
Wigeon *Anas penelope*
Woodcock *Scolopax rusticola*
Wood sandpiper *Tringa glareola*
Yellow wagtail *Motacilla flava*

MAMMALS

Badger *Apodemus mystacinus*
Beaver *Castor fiber*
Elk (American: moose) *Alces alces*
Ermine *Mustela erminea*
Fox *Vulpes vulpes*
Hazel dormouse *Muscardinus avellanarius*
Hare *Lapus capensis*
Hedgehog *Erinaceus algirus*
Muskrat *Ondatra zibethicus*
Northern birch mouse *Sicista betulina*
Otter *Lutra lutra*
Pygmy shrew *Suncus etruscus*
Raccoon dog *Nyctereutes procyonoides*
Red deer *Cervus elephus*
Roe deer *Capreolus capreolus*
Root vole *Microtus raticeps*
Stone marten *Martes foina*
Water shrew *Neomys fodiens*
Wild boar *Sus scrofa*
Wolf *Canis lupus*

FISH

Bleak *Alburnus alburnus*
Bream *Abramis brama*
Burbot *Lota lota*
Chub *Leuciscus cephalus*
Crucian carp *Carassius carassius*
Gudgeon *Gobio gobio*
Ide *Leuciscus idus*
Lampern *Lampetra fluviatilis*
Minnow *Phoxinus phoxinus*
Pike *Esox lucius*
Roach *Rutilus rutilus*
Rudd *Scardinius erytrophthalmus*

Stone loach *Noemachellus barbatulus*
Tench *Tinca tinca*
Wels *Silurus glanis*

AMPHIBIANS

Agile frog *Rana dalmatina*

REPTILES

Sand lizard *Lacerta agilis*

INVERTEBRATES

Insects:
  Lace-winged fly *Chrysopa septempunctata*
  Water damsel *Agrion splendens*

Butterflies:
  Comma butterfly *Polygonia c-album*
  Map butterfly *Araschnia levana*
  Night peacock *Satturnia pallonia*
  Orange tip *Anthocharis cardamines*
  Red admiral *Vanessa atalanta*
  Small copper *Lycaena phlaeas Macroglossum spec.*

Marsh snail *Vivipara vivipara*

Crayfish *Potamobius pallipes*

PLANTS

Alternate-leaved saxifrage *Crysosplenium alternifolium*
Alder *Alnus glutinosa*
Birch *Betula spec.*
Bitter milkwort *Polygala amala*
Bogbean or marsh trefoil *Menyanthes trifoliata*
Bulrush or reed-mace *Typha latifolia*
Common frogbit *Hydrocharis morsus-ranae*
Common horsetail *Equisetum sepc.*
Cuckoo flower or Lady's smock *Cardamine pratensis*
Dandelion *Taraxacum officinale*
Daisy *Bellis perennis*
Dragonroot or Marsh calla *Calla palustris*
Field bugloss *Anchusa arvensis*
Field pansy *Viola tricolor*
Field woodrush *Luzula palustris*
Forget-me-nots *Myosotis arvensis*
Greater pond sedge *Carex ripornia*
Hairy speedwell *Veronica spec.*
Horsetail *Equisetum fluviatile*
Lady's smock *Cardamine pratensis*
Marsh marigold *Caltha palustris*

Marsh trefoil or bogbean *Menyanthes trifoliata*
Marsh violet *Viola or Hottonia palustris*
Mint *Mentha arvensis*
Moss *spec.*
Reed-mace or bulrush *Typha latifolia*
Reeds *Phragmites spec.*
Riverine water crowfoot *Ranunculus fluitans*
Sallow *Salix caprea*
Sedge *Carex spec.*
Spotted orchid *Dactylhoriza majalis*
Spruce *Picea spec.*
Stork's Bill *Geranium spec.*
Yellow deadnettle *Lamiastrum galeobdonom*
Water avens *Geum rivale*
Water lily (white) *Nymphaea alba* (yellow) *Nuphar luteum*
Water mint *Mentha aquatica*
Watersoldier *Stratoites aloides*
Wild strawberry *Galium palustris*
Willow *Salix spec.*
White mouse-eared chickweed *Cerastium spec.*
Wood angelica *Angelica sylvestris*

Portrait of a Living Marsh is a publication of Inmerc BV Wormer, the Netherlands, in cooperation with Artists for Nature Foundation and World Wide Fund for Nature.

The author wants to express his thanks to Etha Brouwers-Elink Schuurman, John Busby and his father Victor Shillcock for their comments and suggestions concerning the text.
He also wants to thank Magnus Sylvén and Adlai J. Amor of WWF International in Gland, Switzerland, and Krzysztof Wolfram of the Office of the Green Lungs of Poland Agreement, in Bialystok, Poland.
For their prompt and generous cooperation thanks to Maciej Zimowski and Eugeniusz Sokol of Bird Service Tourist Agency in Bialystok, and Mr. Przemyslaw Bielicki of the Noth-Podlasie Bird Protection Society, journalist Carla van Lingen of VARA Radio, the Netherlands for access to her tapes containing her interviews of artists taking part in this project, and also Cathma van Dijk and Ysbrand Brouwers, Director of Artists for Nature Foundation.

Artists for Nature Foundation would like to thank the following sponsors:
- Grasduinen nature magazine, Haarlem, The Netherlands
- Mill Pond Press, Venice, Florida, U.S.A.
- Landrover and Mann Egerton of Colchester, Essex, England.
- Jan Veldhuizen of Inmerc BV, publishers

© 1993 Inmerc BV

Photography: Fred F. Hazelhoff, unless otherwise stated.
Reproduction photography: Harry Knippers, Tubbergen, the Netherlands.
Design: Erik Uitenbogaard, bNO (B&U projects, Utrecht, the Netherlands).
Maps: Erik d'Ailly, Amsterdam, the Netherlands.
Production: Inmerc BV, Wormer.

This book is printed on chlorinefree paper.

ISBN 90 6611 053 8
NUGI 825, 921
CIP